IC NIC
C O L L E C T O R S
Where Passion Meets Timeless Value

Collecting the Past, Investing in the Future:

A Handbook on Memorabilia and Its Emergence as an Asset Class

by
BY ICONIC COLLECTORS

Featuring Bobby Rakhit
Founder, Rakhit Capital

Visual Materials Notice:
All images, photographs, and graphics used in this publication are either in the public domain or are proprietary in nature.

Legal Disclaimer:
The information provided in this book is for educational and entertainment purposes only. Every effort has been made to ensure the content is accurate, complete, and up to date. However, no warranties of any kind, express or implied, are made. The author and publisher disclaim all liability for any direct or indirect loss or damages arising from the use or misuse of the information presented, including but not limited to errors, omissions, or inaccuracies.

The reader is solely responsible for their own actions, decisions, and results. This book does not constitute legal, financial, medical, or other professional advice. Readers are encouraged to seek guidance from a licensed professional before acting on any information contained herein.

By reading this document, the reader agrees that under no circumstances shall the author or publisher be held liable for any loss or damage, including but not limited to indirect, special, incidental, or consequential damages.

ISBNs:
Paperback ISBN: 978-1-0684427-8-0

Hardcover ISBN: 978-1-0684427-5-9

eBook (ePub) ISBN: 978-1-0684427-6-6

Audio (ACX) ISBN: 978-1-0684427-7-3

Dedications

To my son, Rohit,

May you always believe that dreams are not just for wishing, but for living.

This book is for you - a small spark to light the way as you begin your own journey of collecting, discovering, and creating a world that's uniquely yours. Always remember that within you lies the power to imagine, to build, and to become.

Follow your passion with heart and courage. Let curiosity guide your steps, and let kindness shape your path, because your story is just beginning.

A special thank you to Ken Goldin.

Your passion for collecting and storytelling has inspired generations, and your work reminds us all that behind everything in existence is a piece of history, a moment, a memory. Thank you for sparking that same sense of wonder in both young collectors and seasoned enthusiasts alike.

Who is Bobby Rakhit?

My name is Bobby Rakhit, and I am a collector.

Over the years, I've curated one of the largest private memorabilia collections in the Middle East, including rare sports artifacts, cultural icons, and historic moments that have shaped generations. Each item I collect tells a story, and collectively, they represent a legacy.

My love for sports is foundational to my collecting. Whether it's the discipline of a championship team, the comeback story of an underdog, or the emotional charge of a final whistle - sports mirror life in every way; that's why I collect. - Not just for rarity or return, but for the emotion, history, and identity embedded in each piece.

Through this book, I aim to reframe how people view memorabilia as 'collectibles' to begin seeing them as an emerging asset class with cultural, emotional, and financial value. This is more than a handbook. It's a guide to seeing value where others see nostalgia.

Professionally, I've always been rooted in finance. I'm proud to be a CFA charter holder, an MBA in Finance graduate, and an alumnus of McGill University. My early career began on the front lines of high finance, working in investment banking and equity research at global institutions like HSBC, U.S. Bancorp, Piper Jaffray, and Morgan Stanley. These experiences laid the foundation for what would become a lifelong passion for markets, value creation, and disciplined investing.

I later took the leap into leadership at FactSet, where I managed sales and consulting across the Middle East, Asia, and Africa, growing not just revenues, but strategic influence in emerging markets. Those achievements helped me establish Rakhit Capital, (https://www.rakhitcapital.com/) a family-run investment vehicle built to grow and preserve wealth through thoughtful, long-term strategies, particularly through alternative opportunities. Our portfolio spans industries including technology, real estate, fintech, and consumer products.

Rakhit Capital is one of the few firms actively developing memorabilia and collectibles as a viable asset class. From rare sports artifacts to culturally iconic items, we believe that alternative investments are not only diversifiers but are storytelling assets with real market potential.

I'm often sharing ideas as a guest lecturer, keynote speaker, and board member across tech and real estate firms, and I regularly contribute to conversations in the press and media, as well as on conference stages. My approach is always hands-on, rooted in structure but open to innovation - especially where investing and culture meet.

About Iconic Collectors

Iconic Collectors (http://iconiccollectors.com) is a global platform and community dedicated to the preservation, authentication, and elevation of culturally significant memorabilia. From game-worn jerseys and championship rings to historic documents and rare collectibles, we celebrate the tangible moments that define history, and help collectors recognize their lasting value.

Founded on the belief that memorabilia is more than nostalgia, Iconic Collectors operates at the intersection of culture, commerce, and capital. We are committed to reimagining investment in memorabilia, blending passion with performance and storytelling with strategy.

We exist to empower collectors, investors, and enthusiasts with the tools, knowledge, and access to build meaningful, high-value collections that appreciate over time - both emotionally and financially.

Prelude

Do you know what's in your attic?

In most homes, the attic is often a quiet, forgotten place- a corner where time seems to stand still. Boxes and crates, stacked high, sit untouched for years, gathering dust and waiting for a moment of rediscovery. We've all been there - sifting through piles of forgotten relics, many of them carrying no more value than the memories of days gone by. Old books, faded photographs, dusty toys, and a thousand other odds and ends that have, over the years, become part of the backdrop of our lives. We tend to forget about them, only occasionally glancing at the collection that's become a quiet record of our own personal history.

But what if, in those forgotten corners, tucked away under layers of dust and cobwebs, were treasures? Items that once seemed insignificant but could now be worth hundreds, thousands, or even millions of dollars. Perhaps your family held onto those items for sentimental reasons - your grandmother's china, your father's baseball cards, or the record player your uncle couldn't bear to part with. For generations, you've stored these objects without giving them much thought, seeing them as pieces of history that are too precious to throw away but not valuable enough to be of any real interest. And yet, in the quiet of these forgotten spaces, great wealth may be waiting to be unearthed.

There's an old saying that a diamond in the rough is hard to find, but sometimes, it's the unassuming item in the attic that can truly shine. "There are some unlikely items in people's attics that can turn out to be valuable," says Nicolas Martin, a flea market expert and founder of Flea Market Insiders. "The odds of finding something valuable in your attic are much higher than winning the lottery!" Think about that. What if you spent just a few hours combing through those forgotten treasures in your attic and uncovered something you had no idea was worth a fortune? It might be an old comic book that's suddenly in demand, or a vintage toy from a beloved franchise that collectors are scrambling for. It could even be something as simple as an old coin or a rare piece of art you inherited. The possibilities are endless.

Consider the case of Martyn Tovey, a man from Radstock, Somerset, who holds the Guinness World Record for the largest collection of Guinness World Record memorabilia. In February 2024, Tovey's incredible collection of 3,089 unique items- from record-breaking certificates to promotional materials- earned him the accolade. But this isn't just an obsessive collector's hobby- it's proof that memorabilia can hold value well beyond what one might expect; while the monetary value of his collection is not publicly disclosed, it is suspected to be in the region of £50,000, minimum. Tovey's collection isn't his only claim to fame; he also holds the record for the largest collection of Guinness World Records annuals - 816 of them, to be exact, some dating back to the very first edition, gifted to him in 1968. The sheer scope of his collection speaks to the power of memorabilia as a time capsule of our shared history, and its surprising potential as a financial asset.

Tovey's collection is just one example; the world of memorabilia is vast, and it includes a wide range of items that can be worth far more than we realize. So, what kinds of items tend to fetch the highest prices? For starters, sports memorabilia. Think jerseys worn by famous athletes, vintage baseball cards, and equipment signed by legendary players. One of the most famous sales in this category was a 1952 Mickey Mantle card *(Plate 1.1)* that sold for over $12 million at Heritage auctions in 2022. The sale shattered previous records and was only surpassed in 2023 by a Babe Ruth's 1932 World Series jersey *(Plate 1.2)*, which fetched $24.12 million. Imagine that!

Beyond sports, classic cars, coins, watches and art have also reached astronomical prices at auction. In 2018, a 1962 Ferrari 250 GTO *(Plate 1.3)* sold for $48.4 million at an RM Sotheby's auction in Monterey, California making it one of the most expensive cars ever sold publicly (more on this later). In a 1933 Double Eagle gold coin *(Plate 1.4)*, which sold for $18.9 million at Sotheby's in New York in 2021, setting a world record for a coin at auction. Vintage watches have also seen soaring demand; a Rolex Daytona owned by Paul Newman sold for $17.8 million at Phillips in 2017. In the art world, Leonardo da Vinci's *Salvator Mundi (Plate 1.5)* sold for $450.3 million at Christie's in New York in 2017, the most ever paid for a work of art. Across categories, collectors consistently seek out items that are rare, in pristine condition, or possess undeniable historical significance.

Many people assume that collecting memorabilia is reserved for the ultra-wealthy. It's easy to believe that only the top 1% have the resources to buy and invest in rare, valuable items. After all, the headlines are often dominated by multi-million-dollar sales and celebrity collectors. However, the truth is that you don't have to be a billionaire to dive into the world of memorabilia and start building your collection. In fact, the market for memorabilia has grown exponentially, with more accessible entry points than ever before. The rise of online auctions, specialized dealers, and even social media platforms dedicated to niche collectibles, means that anyone with an eye for opportunity can start investing in memorabilia, often for far less than one might expect.

You truly don't need to be part of the global elite to make a meaningful investment in memorabilia; there is a way to leverage the passion for collecting not just as a hobby, but as a legitimate investment. The truth is, there's never been a better time to explore memorabilia than now. From limited-edition sneakers and rare concert posters to vintage video games and iconic movie props, there are countless items out there waiting to be discovered - and many of them are far more affordable than you might think.

That's where this book comes in. *Collecting the Past, Investing in the Future* is your guide to understanding everything about memorabilia. It's not just about the thrill of the hunt; it's about understanding how to approach memorabilia as an investment, identifying valuable items, and building a collection that could not only be meaningful to you but potentially profitable as well. This handbook will provide you with the tools and knowledge to navigate the often-overwhelming world of collectibles, helping you discern what's worth investing in and how to approach the market with confidence.

Over the course of this book, we'll explore the different types of memorabilia and collectibles and discuss the factors that influence their value, the impact of trends on the market, and how to assess the authenticity and condition of an item before purchasing. You'll also see loads of statistics and figures about the present market as well as what the future holds (keep in mind that all statistics, data, and figures referenced in this book are accurate to our knowledge as of the time of writing and will potentially change over time).

For many, collecting is a passion - a way to hold onto pieces of history that connect us to the past. But as more and more people begin to understand the financial potential of memorabilia, the line between hobby and investment becomes increasingly blurred. This book will help you tap into that potential, giving you a deeper understanding of how memorabilia can serve as both a window to the past and a wise financial choice for the future.

As you read through these pages, you'll begin to see the world of memorabilia not as an exclusive realm reserved for the wealthiest collectors, but as a vibrant, accessible marketplace where everyone from seasoned investors to enthusiastic newcomers, can uncover hidden treasures, invest in history, and potentially reap significant rewards. The forgotten items in your attic may be the beginning of an exciting journey, and with the right knowledge, you might just be on the verge of discovering a wealth of opportunities waiting to be seized.

Table of Contents

Appendices 195

List of Tables

List of Figures

Part I:
UNDERSTANDING THE COLLECTIBLE MARKET

In 2016, a seemingly ordinary piece of paper sold at Christie's auction for over $200,000. This seemingly innocuous piece of paper was in fact a concert ticket for The Beatles at the Cavern Club in Liverpool, where the legendary band first gained international fame. While many might dismiss such an item as insignificant, to collectors it represents a pivotal moment in music history. The ticket's sale price is proof that an unassuming object, when tied to a significant event, can command staggering value, thanks to its emotional and cultural importance. This is the magic of memorabilia: an ordinary item becomes extraordinary when it's connected to something momentous, making it highly desirable to collectors and investors alike.

The Oxford dictionary defines the term collectible as any item that people seek out, buy, and preserve because of its value, rarity, or historical significance. Memorabilia is a subset of collectibles that refers to objects connected to a particular event, person, or moment in time - often with emotional or cultural importance. Memorabilia can include autographed jerseys, tickets from historic games, or items that capture the essence of an event.

In fact, anything that you assign value can become memorabilia. In December 2005, after the FIFA World Cup draw in Leipzig, Germany, Matthias Blume- a German man working as part of the cleanup crew- noticed the name tags representing the 32 countries had been left behind. Recognizing an opportunity, Blume grabbed the tag for "Germany" and auctioned it off on eBay. Before FIFA could intervene, bids had already surpassed $1,000, showing how even an overlooked item like a name tag could be worth a small fortune to collectors. The name tags became memorabilia because of the value Matthias and later, the buyers assigned them.

2017, a man name Richard Gooding, who at the time worked at a Scottish distillery, stumbled upon a rare bottle of Macallan whisky (*Plate 1.6*) in the back of a storeroom. He had no idea of its value at first, but after a bit of research, he realized it was an extremely rare 1926 Fine & Rare Macallan - one of only 40 bottles produced. He decided to auction it off, and in 2019, the bottle sold for an astounding $1.9 million at Sotheby's, breaking the world record for the most expensive bottle of whisky ever sold (the record was since broken in 2023 by the sale of $2.7 million for a similar bottle). What began as an unnoticed find turned into a treasure trove of profit.

In 2018, a letter written by Vincent van Gogh to his brother Theo, one of the most famous personal communications from the artist, was discovered by an art historian at a small auction house. The letter had been in the private hands for years, passed down through generations, with little recognition for its importance. Once authenticated at Sotheby's, it was sold for over $1 million, becoming an incredibly valuable piece of art memorabilia - demonstrating how the right discovery at the right time can lead to a windfall.

There are countless stories like this, of how seemingly ordinary items become valuable treasures. Whether through a bit of luck, a keen eye, or simply being in the right place at the right time, almost anyone can start collecting and potentially profit from the ever-evolving collectible market.

2023 estimates by Grand View Research place the global market for collectibles at $294 billion and it is still growing. The same research projects a compound annual growth rate of 5.5% in the years leading to 2030 potentially bringing the value to $427.68 billion (Grand View, 2023). These estimates include everything from sports memorabilia, rare toys, art, and vintage items to more niche markets such as comic books, stamps, and even limited-edition sneakers. While these figures are simply estimates- there is a lot of grey matter because many transactions are between individuals and go unrecorded- the sports memorabilia sector alone has already seen exponential growth, with items like autographed jerseys or game-used equipment reaching values in the millions (See Chapter 2). Likewise, other areas such as fine wine, whisky, and luxury watches are rapidly becoming lucrative markets for collectors and investors alike.

What's even more exciting, is that with the rise of online auction platforms and dedicated marketplaces, the ability to start a collection - or even make a profitable investment - has become more accessible than ever. You don't need to be an expert to get involved. Many successful collectors have started with no more than a passion for the subject matter and an eye for value thanks to increased access to information and the democratization of the market.

The first part of this book will help you see how the currently US-led collectible market has evolved over time to become what it is today. The first chapter will provide a history of the collectible market, the second will zoom in on memorabilia and the different types available for you to consider and the third chapter will discuss the market dynamics within the collectible and memorabilia market to set the stage for helping you make memorabilia an investment. Whether you're a first-time investor, a long-time collector, or simply a passionate fan, this part will be a goldmine.

Tyrannosaurus Rex Skull **Source:** *Pediaa.com*	Mask of Tutankhamun **Source:** *Wikipedia*	Abraham Lincoln Portrait **Source:** *Wikipedia*
Roman Tetradrachm coin **Source:** *Picryl.com*	1934 Lincoln Model KB **Source:** *Wikimedia Commons*	Star Wars Stormtrooper Helmet **Source:** *Wikimedia Commons*
Ferrari 250 GTO **Source:** *Wikimedia*	Aston Martin DB4 Series IV **Source:** *Wikimedia*	1997-98 Michael Jordan Card **Source:** *Beckett*

A Brief History of Collectibles

KEY INSIGHTS

- Collecting has long been intertwined with status, legacy, and cultural significance. It is not just about ownership. It's also about preserving identity and memories.

- Innovations - from auction houses to mass media, and later the internet -have continuously expanded access and democratized participation. Today, digital technology and NFTs are redefining ownership and introducing a new frontier of collectibles beyond the physical world.

- Collectibles are increasingly getting recognized as alternative investments and inflation hedges, blending passion with potential financial gain.

Collecting has always been more than just amassing things. At its heart, it's about holding on to pieces of the past that speak to us in deeply personal ways. Whether it's a rare item from your childhood, a token from a legendary event, or something that simply brings back a flood of memories, collectibles have a unique power to connect us with history, and when those items you collect carry emotional weight or cultural significance, they are classified as memorabilia.

All memorabilia are collectibles, but not all collectibles are memorabilia. While this section will discuss collectibles as a whole, the rest of this book will focus on memorabilia, which is why I labor to make the distinction early on. Many people think of memorabilia as items linked to famous events or celebrities, but the truth is that the term has expanded over time. The term "memorabilia" comes from the Latin Memoria, meaning "memory" and true to form, early memorabilia were about memory. Over centuries, it's come to represent all sorts of objects - anything that holds a piece of our personal history or a significant moment in time.

What makes memorabilia and collectibles so compelling - so valuable - is the story behind them. It's not just about the item itself but about the history it holds. A concert ticket from a legendary show, an autographed jersey from a champion athlete, a postcard from a world-changing event, all of these things connect us to the people, moments, and places that have shaped our lives and our world.

What's incredible is that no two pieces are exactly alike. Even if you're holding a mass-produced item, the circumstances surrounding its creation or its ownership could make it one of a kind. That's why it's hard to define a universal standard for what makes something valuable. When we talk about collectibles, we're not just looking at condition or rarity (though those matter, too), we're also seeking out the intangible: the personal or cultural significance that gives an item meaning.

This unique connection to our memories, desires, and history is what drives the value of collectibles. Sometimes, it's difficult to predict what will catch the collective imagination - why does a simple name tag from a famous event sell for $1000, or a seemingly ordinary toy rocket ship become the holy grail for collectors? The answer lies in the story and how that story resonates with people. It's about understanding not just the object but the context in which it exists, and why it strikes a chord with those who seek it out.

So, how did we get here? How did we shape a world where a nametag, a bottle of whisky or a letter by an artist, become so highly coveted, and how can you, too, benefit from collectibles?

Origins and Early Collectibles

From the dawn of human history, people have been drawn to objects that hold meaning and connect us to the past, to milestones in our lives, and even to the very essence of who we are. I'm talking about the things that transcend simple function: the mementos, tokens, and treasures that tell stories and preserve memories. And while "memorabilia" might sound like something modern, its roots stretch back to the earliest days of human existence. Let's take a journey through time and see how the fascination with collecting evolved from prehistoric times to today's vibrant, global market.

The Dawn of Personal Keepsakes

Long before written history, humans were already collecting items that were important to them - objects with both practical uses and symbolic meaning. In those early days, these objects were simple: tools, bones, ornaments. But they held value far beyond their function; a finely crafted stone tool, a rare bone artifact, these weren't just objects. They were mementos of survival, achievements, or rites of passage. They were also passed down through generations, carrying the weight of history and connecting one person to the next.

Picture an exquisitely crafted stone tool from the Paleolithic era for example. One such item - a flint hand axe

- was found in 2015 at a site in England *(Plate 1.7)*. This tool, which dates back around 400,000 years, would be incredibly valuable today not just for its age and rarity but for its historical significance in understanding early human craftsmanship. Such an item could easily fetch several thousand dollars, depending on the market and demand from museums or collectors interested in prehistoric artifacts. (The Paleolithic flint hand axe from Norfolk, UK, dating approximately 400,000 to 150,000 years ago, sold for £8,820 at Sotheby's.)

And we can move even deeper into the past - millions of years rather than thousands back – as another extraordinary category of collectibles emerges: dinosaur fossils. These awe-inspiring relics of prehistoric life, often classified as natural history memorabilia, have become some of the most valuable and contested items ever to appear at auction.

In October 2020, a nearly complete Tyrannosaurus rex skeleton nicknamed "Stan" *(Plate 1.8)* was sold at Christie's in New York for a staggering $31.8 million. Measuring 13 feet tall and over 40 feet long, Stan was discovered in South Dakota in 1987 and was one of the most complete T. rex specimens ever unearthed. The sale, which broke all previous records for dinosaur fossils, eventually led to the fossil's new home at the Natural History Museum, Abu Dhabi.

Before Stan, the record was held by another T. rex, "Sue," whose skeleton was acquired by the Field Museum in Chicago for $8.36 million back in 1997. In more recent years, other ancient predators, such as a 77-million-year-old Gorgosaurus, have also entered the private market, commanding prices well into the millions. These sales, while thrilling, are not without controversy. Many paleontologists have raised ethical concerns, arguing that such significant specimens should remain in public institutions where they can be preserved, studied, and appreciated by all.

In response, some countries have implemented strict regulations or outright bans on fossil exports, treating them as scientific treasures rather than private commodities. Still, the allure of owning a creature that roamed the Earth tens of millions of years ago continues to captivate collectors around the globe. When the Guennol Lioness *(Plate 1.9)* - a 3.25-inch Mesopotamian sculpture dating back to around 3000 BCE - was sold at Sotheby's in 2007 for a staggering $57.2 million, it marked one of the highest prices ever paid for an ancient artifact.

Roman sculptures have also commanded eye-watering sums, such as the marble statue *Artemis and the Stag*, which sold for $28.6 million at Heritage auctions, setting a record at the time for a Roman piece. Even items never sold, like the *Artemision Bronze,* a Greek statue of either Zeus or Poseidon, are considered culturally priceless, with estimated values reaching into the hundreds of millions were they ever to hit the market. Most of these artifacts are protected by cultural heritage laws and museum holdings, but these rare moments of sale give us a glimpse into their monetary value.

The famous "Rosetta Stone", now housed at the British Museum, was bought by the British in 1802 for a small sum of £2,000 (equivalent to around £200,000 today). Had it been offered at auction today, it would likely command hundreds of millions of dollars. The *Rosetta Stone* helped scholars decipher Egyptian hieroglyphs, representing a momentous breakthrough in understanding an ancient civilization.

These items - tools, bones and ornaments - might have been markers of a great hunt or a spiritual ritual, and they often held deep cultural significance. A beautifully carved bone might not only show the skill of the maker but also serve as a symbol of identity or status. Early humans understood the power of these objects, they weren't just useful, they were meaningful. They linked people to their ancestors, their communities, and even to the divine. These objects were more than tools-they were treasures, holding both personal and cultural value. In many cases, early humans believed these items had magical powers bringing good luck, offering protection, or influencing their future. The act of collecting was as much about safeguarding well-being as it was about remembering and honoring the past.

This fascination with ancient relics is not just a modern-day phenomenon; the idea of treasure hunts, legendary items, and high-stakes auctions has been cemented in pop culture thanks to movies like the *Indiana Jones* series, which vividly portrayed the pursuit of rare and valuable treasures. The series brought this fascination to the forefront, portraying fictional but historically rooted treasures like the Ark of the Covenant and the Holy Grail. While these specific artifacts are of course fictional, they mirror the real-world allure of treasures connected to legend. Films like these have inspired generations to hunt for, collect, and protect valuable relics, in some cases driving the prices of similar artifacts into the millions.

This same sense of treasure hunting is now a central theme in *King of Collectibles: The Goldin Touch*, a Netflix series that follows Ken Goldin and his team as they auction some of the world's rarest and most valuable memorabilia. Just as Indiana Jones captivated audiences with his quests for ancient treasures, The Goldin Touch showcases the excitement and high-stakes world of collecting, where items like a signed Michael Jordan jersey or Babe Ruth's contract can fetch millions. The show brings this treasure-hunting spirit to modern-day collectibles, highlighting the intense passion and incredible value behind items that hold a special place in history, culture, and the hearts of collectors.

In 2011, a treasure hunter named Mel Fisher discovered a cache of gold and silver coins valued at $450 million (by experts working with Fisher) from the wreck of the Spanish galleon Nuestra Señora de Atocha, which sank in 1622 off the coast of Florida. These priceless treasures, which included gold bars and jewels, had been lost for nearly 400 years, but the find exemplified the type of high-stakes exploration that has captivated treasure hunters for centuries.

Symbols of Status and Legacy

As human societies began to settle and form more complex structures, the nature of what people collected shifted. With the rise of agriculture, the accumulation of wealth became more possible, and with it came the desire to own items that reflected one's power, status, and achievements.

In ancient civilizations - Mesopotamia, Egypt, the Indus Valley - people began to collect objects not just for their usefulness, but as expressions of prestige. Rulers and warriors started collecting and commissioning rare, beautiful objects such as jewelry, statues, and ornate tools, which reflected their influence or divine favor. These items were more than practical tools; they served as status markers and heirlooms, passed down through generations as symbols of family legacy.

Imagine a finely crafted bronze sword, handed down in a family of warriors, or an intricately designed pottery piece inscribed with royal symbols - these objects were not just valuable; they were tangible links to a person's lineage and legacy. Collecting these items wasn't just about wealth; but about preserving one's place in history.

Throughout the Dark Ages and the Middle Ages, the nature of collectibles evolved yet again - this time through the lens of religion and royalty. Relics, which were often believed to be personal items of saints, kings, or religious figures, became some of the most prized objects of the time. These relics weren't just collectibles, they were believed to hold divine power, drawing pilgrims and admirers from across the land.

A prime example is the *Shroud of Turin*, *(Plate 1.11)* a linen cloth believed by some to be the burial shroud of Jesus Christ. Though its authenticity is debated, the shroud has been revered for centuries and attracts millions of visitors annually. It has immense historical and religious significance and could be worth tens of millions of dollars if it were ever sold on the open market.

Today, ancient Egyptian jewelry is some of the most sought-after collectibles. A notable example is the Mask of Tutankhamun, which was discovered in 1922 by archaeologist Howard Carter in the tomb of the young pharaoh Tutankhamun. The mask, made of gold and inlaid with semi-precious stones, is worth millions - its estimated value is around $10 million, though it's housed in the Egyptian Museum in Cairo and is not for sale. However, items of similar status, like small personal ornaments or pottery from royal tombs, can still fetch staggering amounts. A necklace dating back to the reign of the Pharaohs could easily sell for hundreds of thousands of dollars today.

In 2019, a 22-inch-long Egyptian necklace made of gold and featuring carved scarabs and faience beads, was sold at Sotheby's auction for $2.3 million. This necklace, which dated back to the Late Period of ancient Egypt (circa 600 BC), became one of the most expensive pieces of Egyptian jewelry ever sold at auction. The necklace had been preserved with remarkable detail and is an extraordinary example of the opulence and craftsmanship that characterized Egypt's royal jewelry. A gold and gemstone ring from the Ptolemaic period (circa 200 BC) fetched $1.1 million at Christie's Auction House in 2016. This ring, which bore the image of an ancient Egyptian deity, was among several high-value items from a private collection of ancient Egyptian artifacts.

This tradition of collecting as a display of heritage and prestige continues into the modern era, perhaps most visibly in the British royal family. The Crown Jewels, housed in the Tower of London, are among the most famous royal collections in the world, featuring the 530-carat Cullinan I diamond and the 105-carat Koh-I-Noor, both set into crowns worn by generations of monarchs. These pieces are considered priceless national treasures, but their individual market value would almost certainly run into the hundreds of millions.

In fact, royalty played a key role in the growth of the memorabilia tradition. Kings and queens commissioned elaborate items - crowns, swords, royal garments - not just as functional objects, but as physical representations of power, divine right, and political legacy. These items weren't just for show; they carried an immense weight of symbolism, and during the rise of chivalric orders, knights would collect items like shields and swords as symbols of their honor and achievements, which would be passed down through generations, preserving their status long after their time.

The iconic St. Edward's Crown, among other artifacts, was collected by monarchs over the centuries. While these items are housed in museums and are priceless, similar items associated with royal lineages or noble families have fetched incredible sums in auctions. In 2013, a rare medieval *King Henry VIII pendant* was sold for more than 2.5 million pounds (approximately $4 million at the time) at Sotheby's London auction.

Even in the modern day, Royal family members pass down heirlooms that have become culturally iconic: Princess

Diana's sapphire engagement ring, now worn by Catherine, Princess of Wales, is estimated to be worth over $500,000, though its emotional and symbolic value far exceeds that. Queen Elizabeth II's jewelry collection alone was estimated to be worth at least $110 million at the time of her death, including brooches, tiaras, and necklaces with centuries of royal provenance. These objects are not only beautiful, but they are also deeply woven into the story of Britain itself, reinforcing identity, continuity, and legacy through generations.

The Renaissance and the Rise of Collectors

Then came the Renaissance - an age of rediscovery and cultural renewal. This period marked a turning point for the concept of collecting. As interest in the classical world grew, wealthy individuals and rulers began to collect art, books, and other objects that linked them to the great civilizations of the past. Pieces of art from ancient Greece and Rome were not just valued for their beauty but became prized possessions that symbolized intellectual and cultural sophistication.

The Renaissance also saw the rise of personal collections of portraits, as royal families and noble elites sought to preserve their image and their family legacy through the works of renowned artists. These portraits weren't just likenesses - they were treasures, capturing the essence of an individual's life and their family's place in history. Think of a famous portrait like *The Portrait of Henry VIII* by Hans Holbein. Before 2018, Holbein was an unknown artist. Then he was discovered and now the portrait is worth over $10 million today.

In many ways, the Renaissance brought the idea of memorabilia full circle: items that not only held cultural and historical value but also embodied personal and family legacies. One of the most valuable objects from this period is the *Mona Lisa*, painted by Leonardo da Vinci. Almost everyone today knows of the Mona Lisa, countless movies have been anchored in that piece of art - a ridiculous sale, a heist, or a counterfeit. It is priceless. There are other Renaissance works, such as manuscripts and sculptures, which have made their way to collectors' hands too. For instance, Christie's facilitated the sale of a rare manuscript by da Vinci - his *Codex Leicester* - in 1994 for $30.8 million, to Bill Gates. Other Renaissance items, like rare artworks or pieces of antique furniture, can still command millions of dollars at auction today.

An Industry is Born

Fast forward to the modern era and collectibles have become a booming industry. No longer just the domain of royals or the ultra-wealthy, collecting has become a global phenomenon, and thanks to mass production in the 19th and 20th centuries, collectibles are now more accessible than ever before.

The early 20th century saw the first major wave of sports collectibles, with baseball cards leading the way. These small cards - once part of a cigarette or gum pack - quickly became hot commodities. One of the most notable cards featured in the Goldin Touch was the earlier referred to 1952 Mickey Mantle Topps card, which sold for over $12 million in 2023. A Babe Ruth rookie card fetched prices upwards of $5 million at the auction. Even modern cards, like a 2003 LeBron James rookie card have seen record sales, with one recently selling for nearly $2 million. As the demand for sports memorabilia grew, so did the market, expanding into jerseys, autographed baseballs, and much more.

Today, memorabilia has exploded into a multi-billion-dollar industry. The sports memorabilia market alone was valued at $27.2 billion in 2025 (Verified Market Research, 2025). Items linked to famous musicians, movie stars, and historical figures regularly fetch staggering prices at auctions. For example, a signed Michael Jordan jersey from his "Flu Game" sold for $10.1 million at a 2022 auction, and a prop lightsaber from *Star Wars* fetched $2.2 million *(Plate 1.12)*, both at Sotheby's.

Once dominated by high-end auction houses like Christie's & Sotheby's, which regularly sold rare and valuable items to the elite, the market has undergone a transformation. The rise of online platforms like eBay has democratized access, allowing anyone with an interest to buy and sell memorabilia. Tech innovations, such as the blockchain for authentication and digital collectibles, have further changed the landscape, making it easier for collectors to acquire rare items that were once out of reach.

Collecting has evolved far beyond a hobby to become a cultural and financial force. What started as a simple human desire to connect with the past has now become a global industry, and you could be a part of it, too. Whether it's sports memorabilia, movie collectibles, or historical artifacts, there's never been a better time to start building your own collection and maybe even uncover the next big thing.

The Role of Auctions in Popularizing Collectibles

As you have seen, collecting is a timeless passion - one that transcends generations, cultures, and continents, and auctions have played a key part more than once, especially after the renaissance. This is because they played a significant role in popularizing collectibles and developing the market. In fact, the auction house, in its many variations, has been the driving force in turning obscure treasures into prized assets, helping to define the value of collectibles in ways that we might never have imagined.

Auctions do more than just sell items; they create an environment where value is revealed through competition, rarity, and desirability. It's a world that draws collectors, investors, and enthusiasts, all eager to get their hands on objects which tell a story and hold lasting significance. Auctions play a pivotal role in unlocking the worth of everything from sports memorabilia and vintage cars to rare wines, stamps, and antique jewelry. Imagine walking into an auction and bidding on a rare item, not knowing it will soon become the centerpiece of your collection and possibly your financial portfolio.

One of the most fascinating examples of auction-driven value comes from an unlikely place - fine wines. For connoisseurs, a bottle of rare wine is much more than just a drink; it's a piece of history and an investment that can appreciate over time. In 2011, a single bottle of *Domaine de la Romanée-Conti* - one of the most coveted wines in the world - was sold at a Sotheby's auction in Hong Kong for $232,000. This bottle was part of a collection owned by a private buyer, who had spent years meticulously curating rare wines from the world's top vineyards. He had acquired this particular bottle many years ago at a relatively modest price, but through the years, its rarity and impeccable provenance only added to its allure. When it came to sell, the wine fetched a record-breaking price. That's the power of auctions; they turn something like a bottle of wine which might have simply been enjoyed for its taste, into a highly valuable collectible that increases in worth as the years go by.

In 2018, another bottle of Domaine de la Romanée-Conti - this time a 1945 vintage - sold at Sotheby's for an astonishing

$558,000. Only 600 bottles were produced just after World War II, and today this Burgundy is regarded as one of the most coveted wines in existence. In November 2023, Sotheby's London sold a bottle of The Macallan 1926 60-Year-Old whisky (Peter Blake label) for a staggering $2.7 million, making it the most expensive spirit ever sold. Although technically whisky, its cultural and collectible status places it in the same elite tier as the world's finest wines. With only 40 bottles ever made, its value lies not just in the contents, but in its scarcity, design, and legacy.

Other historic auction results in this niche include the 1992 Screaming Eagle Cabernet Sauvignon, a cult favorite from Napa Valley, which sold for $500,000 at a charity auction in 2000. Even whisky collectors have their holy grails, such as The Macallan 1926 Michael Dillon edition, hand-painted by the Irish artist and sold in 2018 for $1.53 million. In 2011, a 62-year-old bottle of Dalmore changed hands for around $250,000 at a Singapore airport, showing that even airport lounges have become unexpected venues for high-stakes acquisitions.

Together, these examples reinforce one essential truth: auctions don't just reveal market value - they create it. By turning passion into competition and history into capital, they elevate collectibles from personal indulgences into global assets.

And this is true for any type of collectible; like a stamp for example. While stamps are usually seen as being pretty mundane, they can carry immense value, thanks to auctions. In 2016, a rare British *Penny Black* stamp *(Plate 1.13)* sold at a Sotheby's auction for over $3 million. This iconic stamp, which dates back to 1840, is the world's first adhesive postage stamp and represents a pivotal moment in postal history. It was originally purchased by an avid stamp collector, who had spent years seeking out rare examples of early stamps to complete his collection. After years of careful preservation, the stamp was sold to another passionate collector at auction, who saw past it's obvious historical potential and viewed it as a valuable asset.

Auctions have played a part in all kinds of collectibles including jewelry, toys, antiques and vintage cars. Jewelry has always been a symbol of wealth, status, and timeless elegance. But some pieces have an additional layer of intrigue because of their history. Take, for instance, the famous *Pink Star Diamond*. This stunning 59.60 carat diamond was sold at a Sotheby's auction in 2017 for an eye-popping $71.2 million. The diamond, which was cut from a rough stone discovered in South Africa, had been acquired by an anonymous bidder who had placed it in his collection for several years. What made this piece truly valuable wasn't just its size, but its color and provenance. Once the diamond was sold, it set a new world record for the highest price ever paid for a gemstone at auction.

These kinds of jewelry auctions are more than just sales, they're a way for collectors to acquire not just a beautiful object, but a piece of history that continues to appreciate in value. With each auction, the value of these items can rise exponentially, depending on demand, rarity, and the story behind the piece.

In 2019, a *Steiff Teddy Bear* - one of the first stuffed animals ever made - sold at a German auction for $2.3 million. The bear was originally created in the early 20th century and was part of an extensive collection of vintage dolls and toys. The bear had been owned by a private collector who had acquired it decades before at a small antiques market, unaware of its future worth. Through the years, the collector lovingly preserved the bear, and when it went up for auction, it attracted bidders from all over the world. The high price it fetched wasn't just about its rarity; it was about the story it told - a piece of childhood history that would never be repeated.

Two years later, a rare Cabbage Patch Doll from the 1980s sold at Christie's auction for $200,000. Originally created by artist Xavier Roberts in the late 1970s and made famous in the 1980s, these dolls became a cultural phenomenon. This specific doll had been kept in pristine condition by its original owner, who had purchased it during the height of the Cabbage Patch craze in the mid-'80s. What started as a simple, handmade doll quickly transformed into a symbol of childhood nostalgia and intense consumer demand, with parents scrambling to get their hands on one. This particular doll had been stored carefully in its unopened box, preserving its value as a collectible.

The Barbie doll is another culturally enduring and globally recognized doll collectible. Originally launched in 1959, Barbie has not only remained a toy box staple for generations but also emerged as a serious investment-grade collectible. In 2010, a one-of-a-kind Barbie designed by luxury jeweler Stefano Canturi sold at Christie's for $302,500. The doll was adorned with over three carats of white diamonds and a striking one-carat pink diamond on her neck. The sale not only raised funds for breast cancer research, but also marked a turning point for the brand: Barbie, often dismissed as a child's toy, had entered the high-end collectibles market with serious momentum.

Another notable example came in 1999, when diamond giant De Beers created a Barbie to celebrate the brand's 40th anniversary. Wearing a gown adorned with 160 diamonds, the doll was valued at around $85,000. Meanwhile, original 1959 Barbies - especially the #1 edition in its original box - have sold for up to $27,850. These first-run dolls, featuring the iconic black-and-white swimsuit and ponytail hairstyle, are among the most coveted by collectors.

Barbie's cultural relevance received a major boost with the release of the 2023 *Barbie* movie, starring Margot Robbie and directed by Greta Gerwig. The film sparked a global wave of Barbie nostalgia and renewed interest in vintage and designer editions. Following the film's release, online search interest for collectible Barbies surged, and several limited editions saw price spikes at auctions and private sales. What was once seen as a toy is now widely recognized as a cultural artifact - a symbol of femininity, fashion, and evolving identity - and an asset in its own right.

Similarly, antique furniture and automobiles can fetch staggering prices at auctions. A *Louis XVI Secrétaire* desk from the 18th century sold for over $15 million at a Christie's auction in 2018. At the same time, a Ferrari 250 GTO - one of only 36 ever made - sold for a record $48.4 million at Sotheby's. This rare sports car had been owned by a private collector who acquired it in the 1970s for just a fraction of what it would eventually sell for. Over the years, the car had been lovingly restored and maintained, making it even more desirable to buyers.

Just like the stock exchange, auctions facilitate the buying and selling of high-value collectibles, creating a market where prices are determined by the forces of supply and demand. They provide a platform for rare items to find new owners, often commanding top dollar for the privilege of owning a unique piece of history. They bring together buyers and sellers in a high-energy environment where value is assigned in real-time, based on demand and competition. It's not just about what an item is worth to the seller but what it's worth to a group of passionate buyers, each vying for the chance to own it. Keep in mind that the value of these collectibles is not static; it is shaped by the market, and auctions offer the necessary liquidity for these high-value assets to change hands efficiently.

Take the sale of *Michael Jordan's game-worn sneakers* at a 2020 Sotheby's auction, which sold for $1.472 million. These sneakers, worn during Jordan's 1984 rookie season, were originally obtained by a private collector from a charity event where Jordan had signed the sneakers. The collector held onto them for decades, unsure of their value, but was pleasantly surprised at the auction.

In all these examples, auctions demonstrate that value is determined by more than just rarity. The excitement, the history, the provenance- all of these factors play into the final price. Auctions bring a sense of urgency and competition, which elevates the value of these items beyond what many could ever anticipate and goes a long way into turning everyday objects into treasures. Whether you're interested in collecting wine, sports cards, movie star memorabilia, stamps, vintage cars, or rare antiques, auctions provide the perfect platform to start your collection.

Key Milestones in the Growth of the Collectible Market

The market for collectibles has witnessed an extraordinary transformation over the past century, evolving from a niche interest into a global, multi-billion-dollar industry. Here are some of the milestones that have shaped the evolution of the collectibles market:

1. Barter, religion and superstition

Before the formal market for memorabilia existed, societies used objects as symbols of power, wealth, and belief. The earliest forms of "collectibles" were often seen in the context of barter; people traded objects of perceived value such as food, livestock, or rare materials. Over time, certain objects gained symbolic meaning, especially within religious contexts. Sacred artifacts or relics were often regarded as more than simple possessions- they were considered embodiments of divine power, worthy of admiration and reverence. This early association of objects with power, superstition, and belief set the stage for future markets of collectability.

2. Collecting as a show of wealth

As societies began to form complex hierarchies, the role of material possessions shifted. The wealthy and elite began to collect items that showcased their power, status, and legacy. Kings, queens, and emperors were known for amassing collections of rare and priceless objects, from ancient armor to precious jewels, with many passed down through generations. These early collections were not just about ownership, they were about creating a lasting legacy.

Take the case of Sotheby's 2007 auction, which sold a collection of rare royal jewelry that belonged to the late Princess Diana for $6.5 million. but the stunning pieces weren't just valuable for their diamonds or sapphires however, they carried the history of one of the most beloved figures of the 20th century. That's what makes collecting so compelling: you're not just holding an object, but the story behind it.

3. Agoras, marketplaces and the rise of auction houses

In ancient Greek agoras and bustling Roman markets, traders began to formalize the exchange of rare goods, laying the foundation for modern auction houses. Fast forward to the 20th century, and the establishment of iconic auction houses like Sotheby's and Christie's created a formal space for rare and valuable objects to be bought and sold, driving up their value. Auctions provided the perfect setting for collectors and investors to compete for rare items, ensuring fair market values and fueling the passion of those who wished to own something extraordinary.

4. The birth of sports memorabilia market

In the 1920s and 1930s, the sports world began to professionalize, and with it the collectible market for sports memorabilia. Baseball cards, once sold as a simple promotional item with gum or cigarettes, became the cornerstone of sports collecting. Over time, the scarcity of certain cards, like the *1909 Honus Wagner T206*, skyrocketed in value, setting the stage for the booming market, valued at $27.2 billion in 2023 (Verified Market Research, 2024).

Fast forward to today, and sports memorabilia has become an industry in its own right. In 2022, Michael Jordan's game-worn jersey from his 1998 NBA finals 'last dance' fetched an eye-popping $10.1 million at Sotheby's. The beauty of this market is that you don't need to be a seasoned investor to dive in, you can start with relatively low-cost items like limited edition trading cards and gradually work your way up to owning historically significant items such as jerseys or even championship rings.

5. Television, radio and mass communication

The 1950s marked the rise of television, bringing the entertainment world into millions of homes and making sports figures, movie stars, and musicians household names. This new medium gave fans unprecedented access to their favorite stars, and collecting memorabilia became a way to feel connected to those figures. Iconic moments from film and television captured the public's imagination, leading to the rise of collectible items tied to these stars. An example of this is Marilyn Monroe's famous white dress from *The Seven Year Itch, which instantly* became an object of desire, eventually selling for $5.6 million at Christie's in 1999. As radio and television became central to mass communication, the collectibles market grew in tandem, feeding a public fascination with celebrity and historical pop culture.

6. The internet revolution

The 1990s marked a seismic shift in the collectibles landscape with the rise of the internet. For the first time, collectors weren't confined to garage sales, flea markets, or specialty stores; they could connect globally. This digital transformation made collecting more accessible, transparent, and scalable. Hobbyists and serious investors alike could now participate in auctions, communities, and private trades across continents with just a few clicks.

The internet also shifted the mindset around collectibles. No longer just passion projects, they began evolving into serious investment vehicles. As interest grew, platforms like Rally Rd. and Otis emerged, offering fractional ownership in high-end collectibles, from million-dollar sports cards to vintage Porsches. These platforms allowed regular investors to own shares in rare, valuable items, democratizing access to an elite asset class once reserved for the ultra-wealthy.

Meanwhile, global economic instability and inflation concerns pushed investors toward tangible assets. Collectibles gained newfound appeal as hedges against currency devaluation. As institutions began to diversify into collectibles, treating them like alternative assets akin to gold or real estate, their status as legitimate financial instruments solidified.

Luxury goods surged in value: Rolex Daytona climbed 50% in a few years, and in 2022 the Patek Philippe Grandmaster Chime sold for $31 million, becoming the most expensive watch ever auctioned. Likewise, Picasso and Basquiat paintings routinely broke the $100 million threshold at Sotheby's and Christie's, reflecting the art market's resilience in turbulent economic times.

7. ebay and online auctions

Before 1995, the world of memorabilia collecting operated in a very different way. Buying and selling were largely confined to elite auction houses like Sotheby's and Christie's, local antique shops, or through private dealers with insider knowledge. Entry into this world often requires significant resources, expertise, and connections. Many niche items such as sports cards, action figures, or retro video games were dismissed as toys or novelties, with no formal marketplace to validate their worth.

There was no centralized system for price discovery, no searchable transaction history, and certainly no mass participation. If you wanted to collect, it meant attending trade shows, calling up dealers, or relying on printed newsletters. Traditional auctions were high-stakes events, limited by geography, and often intimidating for casual buyers.

That all changed in 1995 when eBay launched, redefining what a marketplace could be. It didn't just make buying and selling easier, it democratized the process. Suddenly, anyone with internet access could list a collectible, and anyone around the world could bid on it. Whether it was a 1980s action figure, a misprinted baseball card, or a vintage concert poster, eBay gave these items visibility, liquidity, and value. It didn't just facilitate transactions - it validated the market.

This was eBay's most significant contribution: it transformed collecting from a niche pastime into a global economy. It gave rise to a new type of collector - the casual seller, the part-time flipper, the parent cleaning out the attic - who now had a direct line to buyers across the world. A card stashed away in a Nebraska basement could suddenly end up in a Tokyo display case. Collectibles once limited by geography now had an international stage.

As the platform matured, it gave birth to a powerful cultural shift: the rise of the flipper. No longer was memorabilia collecting solely driven by nostalgia. People began treating collectibles as investment assets. A new generation of entrepreneurs emerged, buying low and selling high. eBay created the infrastructure for this resale culture, blurring the line between collector and investor.

As eBay grew, so did its influence. It became a proving ground for prices, a place to spot trends, and the first major arena where hobbyists and opportunists collided. Items once seen as "junk" gained collector status based on public interest and real-time bidding behavior. Vintage wrestling figures, old sports tickets, early Pokémon cards, once considered throwaway pop culture, began fetching thousands, then tens of thousands of dollars.

This new visibility forced traditional institutions to evolve. Major auction houses began shifting online or partnering with eBay-style platforms to stay relevant. Heritage Auctions, Goldin Auctions, and PWCC emerged as powerhouses, combining eBay's accessibility with high-end authentication and curation. Bidding wars now span continents, with global buyers driving up prices to unprecedented levels.

The rise of online bidding also introduced a layer of trust. Professional grading services like CGC (for comics), PSA (for cards and autographs), and Wata Games (for video games) began assigning official condition scores to collectibles. These scores determined market value and helped prevent fraud, fueling a new level of confidence and professionalism in the trade.

Of course, eBay's openness also created problems, chief among them, counterfeit items- forgeries of autographs and signed memorabilia flooded the site in the early 2000s. But this, too, spurred progress. Third-party authentication services like PSA, Beckett, and JSA rose to meet the challenge, while eBay itself introduced buyer protections and its 'Authenticity Guarantee' for items like watches, sneakers, and trading cards.

Today, online auctions are a billion-dollar business. From rare sneakers to Pokémon cards, collectors track prices through platforms like eBay, Goldin, and PWCC Marketplace, giving everyday enthusiasts access to elite-grade investment opportunities from their living rooms. What began as a peer-to-peer experiment has evolved into a cornerstone of the collectible's economy, redefining who can participate, what holds value, and how modern markets are built. In short, eBay didn't just change how we buy and sell, it changed what we value, and why.

8. NFTs and digital collectibles

In 2021, the art world was stunned when digital artist Beeple's NFT (Non-Fungible Tokens), *"Everydays: The First 5000 Days"*, sold at Christie's for $69.3 million. With that single auction, NFTs became an undeniable force in the collectibles market.

Unlike physical items, NFTs are blockchain-based digital assets, completely unique, trackable, and verifiable. They unlocked a new dimension of collecting that transcended borders and storage issues. You don't need a display case, a vault, or even a physical object, just digital ownership in a decentralized ecosystem.

Celebrities like Tom Brady have embraced the trend. His platform, Autograph, partnered with icons like Tiger Woods and Simone Biles to release exclusive digital collectibles. These collaborations are bringing mainstream attention and credibility to NFTs, attracting everyone from crypto investors to lifelong collectors looking for their next frontier.

Although the NFT market has its ups and downs, it proves that digital ownership could be just as emotionally resonant- and potentially as lucrative- as physical collectibles. Rare gaming NFTs, digital sports cards, music rights, and even virtual real estate are emerging as asset classes.

Behind the scenes, institutional capital has poured in. Hedge funds and private equity firms now view rare collectibles as alternative investments with explosive upside potential. The increasing institutional interest in collectibles is a clear sign of the growing recognition of these items as legitimate assets, mirroring traditional investments like gold, real estate, and stocks. This shift is happening at a time when central banks around the world are flooding markets with fiat currency in response to global economic challenges, resulting in inflation and the devaluation of traditional money. In this uncertain economic environment, many investors are turning to tangible assets that hold enduring value and can act as a hedge against inflation.

Just like gold or silver, which have long been safe havens during times of economic instability, collectibles such as watches, fine art, sports memorabilia, and vintage wines, increasingly seen as attractive investments. These assets are less affected by fluctuations in currency values and more influenced by scarcity, cultural significance, and historical importance. Their appeal as a store of value has only intensified as central banks around the world have pursued aggressive monetary policies to stimulate their economies. Collectibles are becoming a way for investors to safeguard their wealth while diversifying their portfolios.

We are living in a time where the value of currency can fluctuate dramatically. It can become seemingly worthless, just to bounce back by only the faith of the country or government. It's no wonder investors are seeking alternative ways to preserve their wealth. Collectibles are now being seen as more than just sentimental items or niche investments. They are emerging as a viable asset class that can protect against inflation, diversify portfolios, and offer long-term growth potential, no matter what class of memorabilia you're collecting, you're tapping into a market with an ever-growing appetite for rare and unique items. The right piece, purchased at the right time, could not only be a conversation starter in your collection but could also become an asset that appreciates in value, often outpacing traditional investments.

As the lines between passion and investment continue to blur, the world of collectibles offers something unique: the chance to turn an interest or hobby into a lucrative financial opportunity. Whether you're an experienced investor or a beginner looking to dip your toes into a new asset class, there's never been a better time to start building your collection and your wealth.

Types of Collectibles and Memorabilia

KEY INSIGHTS

- The global collectibles market spans diverse categories - sports, entertainment, historical, and pop culture - with valuations reaching into the billions and strong growth projected through 2030.

- Across all categories, scarcity and pristine condition are paramount. Original packaging, first editions, and authenticated items consistently command premium prices.

- Major conventions like San Diego Comic-Con and New York Comic Con are crucial market catalysts, driving fan engagement, unveiling rare items, and expanding collectible ecosystems.

- With blockbuster franchises, streaming shows, and gaming continuing to expand global fandoms, the collectibles market is poised for sustained growth, offering lucrative opportunities for passionate collectors and savvy investors alike.

Clearly, collecting is more than just a hobby. In a collectible, history, emotion, and investment come together in a unique way. From antique furniture that whispers tales of centuries past, to limited edition action figures that remind us of childhood dreams, collectibles have a powerful draw.

There's something exhilarating about owning a piece of the past, something that not only holds sentimental value but can also grow in worth over time.

The collectibles industry is thriving. The global market for collectibles is valued at over $294 billion and is expected to continue growing at a steady pace. According to a report by Grand View Research, the global collectibles market is projected to expand to a CAGR of 5.5% from 2025 to 2030. This growth is driven by increasing consumer interest in rare items, the rise of online auction platforms, and the growing recognition of collectibles as an alternative investment.

The global memorabilia market is valued at over $50 billion as of 2025, with continued growth expected. According to a report by Market Research Future, the memorabilia market is projected to grow at a CAGR of 6.1% from 2025 to 2030. Clearly, the opportunities for collecting are many.

To better understand the scope and diversity of this market, it is useful to categorize the types of items that fall under the umbrella of "collectibles." Collectors are drawn to a wide range of categories, each with their own cultural, historical, or nostalgic appeal. Table 1 below provides a general overview of the most popular categories of collectibles and representative examples within each.

Table 1: Types of Collectibles and Examples

CATEGORY	EXAMPLES
Antiques	Furniture, Clocks, China, Paintings
Art	Paintings, Sculptures, Photography, Prints
Automobilia	Cars, Car Memorabilia, Manuals, Advertisements
Books	First Editions, Signed Copies, Rare Books
Coins	Old Coins, Rare Coins, Mint Errors, Bullion Coins

Comics	Superhero Comics, Manga, Vintage Comics, Limited Editions
Die-cast Models	Cars, Trains, Airplanes, Ships
Entertainment Memorabilia	Posters, Costumes, Scripts, Props, Photographs, Signed Items from Films & TV Shows, Vinyl Records, Cassette Tapes, Autographed Albums, Concert Tickets
Figurines	Action Figures, Dolls, Ceramic Figurines, Miniatures
Nautical	Ship Models, Maritime Artifacts, Navigation Instruments
Stamps	Rare Stamps, Commemorative Stamps
Sports Memorabilia	Jerseys, Balls, Autographed Items, Trading Cards, Tickets, Programs
Video Games	Classic Games, Consoles, Limited Edition Items
Historical & Political Memorabilia	War Artifacts, Military Medals, Presidential Signatures, Political Campaign Items, Documents, Early man artifacts, Dinosaur bones
Pop Culture Memorabilia	Action Figures, Comic Books, Vinyl Records, Limited Edition Toys, Fan Art, Video Games, Teddy Bears, Lego sets

Source: Adapted from Wikipedia, 2025.

As shown in Table 1, the landscape of collectibles is both vast and varied, encompassing everything from ancient artifacts and fine art to pop culture ephemeral and digital-age rarities. Each category represents not only a different segment of the market but also a different emotional and financial motivation for collectors.

Each of these categories is a universe of its own, with the potential to grow in value as the years go by. Whether you're collecting for passion or profit, knowing the ins and outs of each type - from its historical significance to the rarity and condition of the items - is key to making smart choices. You don't have to be an expert, but with a little research, a love for what you collect, and the thrill of discovering rare gems, you can begin your own journey into collectibles.

With the focus of this book on memorabilia, this chapter will consider in depth the major categories of memorabilia available. The global memorabilia market, valued at over $50 billion in 2025, spans four major categories, each contributing uniquely to the overall market. Figure 1 provides a breakdown of the key categories including their estimated market contributions and projected CAGR from 2025 to 2030. This data illustrates not only the current economic significance of each segment but also their future potential as investment-grade assets.

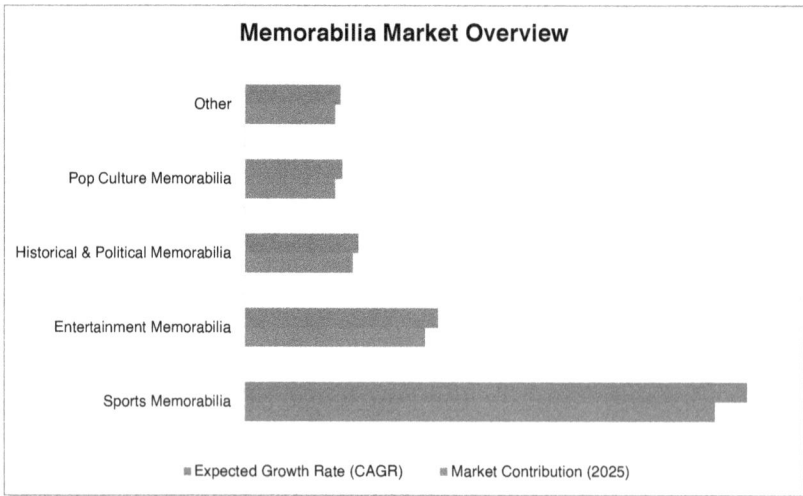

Figure 1: Major Categories of Memorabilia

Source: Market Research Future, 2025; Statista, Grand View Research

As Figure 1 demonstrates, sports memorabilia continue to dominate the market, but pop culture and entertainment memorabilia are showing especially strong growth potential fueled by younger collectors, media influence, and the rise of digital platforms. Historical artifacts, while more niche, hold profound cultural and academic value, often commanding significant premiums at auction.

Sports Memorabilia

Sports memorabilia stands as the largest and most dynamic sector within the collectibles market. The global sports memorabilia market is currently valued at approximately $27.2 billion in 2025 and is projected to reach $32.4 billion by 2031, with a compound annual growth rate (CAGR) of 7.1% during this period. This growth is driven not just by nostalgic collectors, but by an increasingly global fan base and a shift in how these items are perceived - not merely as keepsakes, but as serious alternative investments. Research from Market Decipher also indicates that the North American market alone is expected to grow at 8.9% CAGR from 2025 to 2033, driven in part by expanding digital engagement and the internationalization of sports fandom.

Globalization has had a profound impact on the evolution of the sports memorabilia market. Fans from Asia to South America are now collecting items related to players like Messi, Ronaldo, and LeBron James, whose appeal transcends borders. Sports fandom is no longer local, it's global, and global demand is driving up value. At the same time, collectibles are increasingly being treated as investment vehicles, with platforms like Rally and Collectable offering fractional ownership in rare sports items, allowing average investors to own a share of a game-worn jersey or a historic trading card. The rise of data-driven buying behavior reflects a larger trend toward investment-minded collecting, where emotional value intersects with financial logic.

Technological innovations are also transforming authenticity and trust. Blockchain technology and NFTs now offer immutable provenance, permanently linking a specific item - say, a basketball jersey worn in Game 7 of the Finals - to a digital certificate that confirms its use, reducing fraud and giving buyers greater confidence. Major documentaries and sports-centered streaming content like "The Last Dance," "Beckham," and "Break Point", have reignited public interest in legendary figures and their memorabilia, increasing both emotional and monetary value. When Michael Jordan's "Last Dance" jersey sold for $10 million *(Plate 2.1)*, its connection to a cultural phenomenon amplified the price well beyond traditional estimates.

This environment is also shaped by a cultural shift toward live shopping and the creator economy. Platforms like TikTok, YouTube, and Whatnot have turned memorabilia sales into events. Influencers host live auctions in real time, merging entertainment with commerce and drawing in younger demographics, many of whom now see collectibles not just as nostalgic objects, but as assets to be flipped, tracked, and traded. Athletes themselves are transforming the space, bypassing auction houses and selling memorabilia directly to fans, often via NFTs or curated collections. LeBron James, Tom Brady, and Serena Williams are just a few athletes leveraging this model, blurring the line between athlete, entrepreneur, and cultural brand.

Besides, when respected financial institutions like the CFA Institute begin acknowledging memorabilia as an alternative investment class, it sends a powerful message: this market is no longer operating in the margins. The CFA's involvement gives sports memorabilia a form of institutional credibility that it previously lacked, helping to legitimize the space in the eyes of traditional investors. As sports continue to dominate popular culture- especially through media crossovers and digital exposure- the memorabilia market is not just thriving - it's transforming.

The past was collector-driven and locally focused, while the future is investment-driven, globalized, and authenticated through technology. Sports memorabilia has become a powerful convergence of culture, emotion, and economics, offering opportunities to those who see both the story and the value in every artifact.

It encompasses items associated with athletes, teams, and historic events, often tied to moments of greatness or personal achievement. Sports memorabilia includes (but is not limited to):

- Jerseys – Iconic items like Michael Jordan's jersey from the 1997 NBA Finals or a vintage Babe Ruth jersey.
- Trading Cards – Think of a 1952 Topps Mickey Mantle baseball card, or a LeBron James rookie card. Cards like these are highly sought after, and their value skyrockets when tied to record-breaking players.
- Equipment – Game-used equipment like Babe Ruth's bat, a football signed by the 1972 Miami Dolphins, or Lionel Messi's game-worn cleats. These items hold the memories of unforgettable performances.

Opportunities in the Market

The sports memorabilia market is thriving and evolving, even though some categories are more developed than others. Baseball cards have been a cornerstone of sports memorabilia for decades and the market for these collectibles is well-established, with trusted grading services like PSA (Professional Sports Authenticator) ensuring the authenticity and condition of each item. But sports memorabilia are not just baseball cards anymore.

Jerseys from basketball legends like Michael Jordan and baseball icons like Babe Ruth are skyrocketing in value. When an athlete's career reaches legendary status, the value of their memorabilia can shoot up just as quickly. For example, a signed helmet from NFL star Russell Wilson *(Plate 2.2)* was priced at just $150 early in his career. However, as Wilson led the Seattle Seahawks to victories and garnered more attention, the value of that helmet soared to over $500 as per Hunt auctions listings. The value of sports memorabilia is often closely tied to an athlete's performance, achievements and popularity.

The United States remains the most mature and opportunity-rich market for sports memorabilia, backed by a deeply rooted sports culture, established auction houses, and a robust network of collectors and grading services. The upcoming FIFA World Cup being hosted in the U.S. will serve as a major catalyst, drawing global attention and boosting interest and values across soccer-related memorabilia, especially among new and international collectors.

However, emerging markets are stepping into the spotlight in a big way. Countries and nations like China, India, and the Middle East are showing rapidly growing interest in sports collectibles, driven by rising disposable incomes, increased exposure to international sports, and a new generation of digital-savvy fans. This global momentum is expanding the collector base and driving demand for a wider variety of sport memorabilia, especially as global athletes gain international fame and cross-border appeal. Figure 2 below highlights the sports with the largest fan bases globally in 2025, underscoring the growing international reach of various sports.

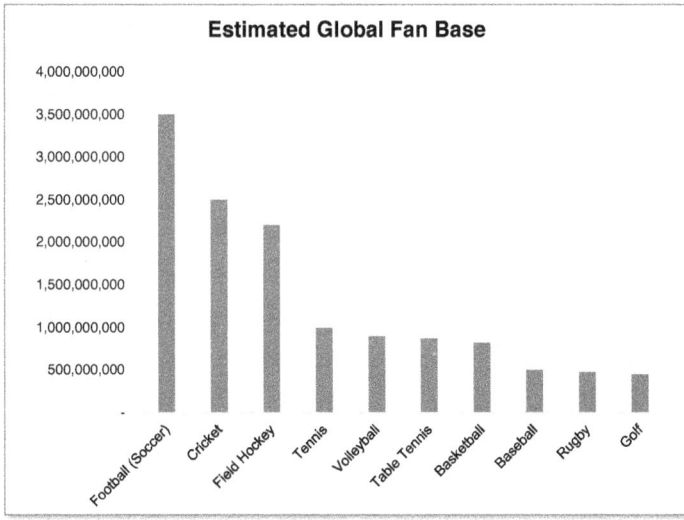

Estimated Global Fan Base

Figure 2: Most Watched Sports in the World

Source: The Athletic Build, 2

Various sports categories exhibit different growth rates, and new opportunities are emerging in previously untapped areas. As the global fan base of sports diversifies and expands, the memorabilia market will continue to experience a shift, with newer sports gaining momentum in the collector space. This growing interest opens the door to new market segments, creating additional potential for growth in sports memorabilia across the world.

- Soccer memorabilia

While baseball and basketball memorabilia have long dominated the scene, soccer memorabilia are emerging as one of the fastest-growing segments in the market - and the United States is quickly becoming a major catalyst in that evolution.

The 2026 FIFA World Cup, set to be hosted across the U.S., Canada, and Mexico, is expected to supercharge interest in soccer collectibles like never before, and this isn't speculation - it's a trend already in motion. With global icons like Lionel Messi now playing in Major League Soccer (MLS), and more international stars expected to follow, the league's rising profile is transforming the U.S. into a legitimate soccer powerhouse - both on the pitch and in the collectibles market.

However- and perhaps unexpectedly- the biggest growth story might just be in women's soccer. The 2023 FIFA Women's World Cup didn't just break records, it was the most-watched TV event in the U.S., outperforming many major sports broadcasts (Forbes, 2023). That kind of exposure is a game-changer. With the rapid rise of leagues such as the English Women's Super League, and the increasing commercial visibility of stars like Alex Morgan, Sam Kerr, and Chloe Kelly, women's soccer memorabilia is becoming a serious investment category in its own right.

Globally, soccer commands a fanbase of over 3.5 billion, and as its influence spreads across the U.S., Asia, and the Middle East, memorabilia tied to historical moments, legendary players, and breakthrough tournaments is gaining serious momentum. Whether it's a Messi Inter Miami jersey, a match-used boot from a Women's World Cup final, or vintage World Cup posters, this is no longer a niche market - it's a tidal wave of opportunity. This is evident from some recent record-breaking soccer memorabilia auction prices

- Diego Maradona's 1986 "Hand of God" Jersey (*Plate 2.3*) - Sold for a record £7.1 million ($9.3 million) at Sotheby's in London in May 2022, making it the most expensive piece of sports memorabilia ever sold at auction.

- Lionel Messi's 2022 World Cup Jerseys - A set of six jerseys worn during Argentina's historic World Cup campaign sold for $7.8 million at an auction held by Sotheby's New York in December 2023.

- Erling Haaland's Rookie Card *(Plate 2.4)* - A PSA 10-graded rookie card of Erling Haaland sold for $125,000, highlighting the surging interest in soccer trading cards.

These record-breaking sales underscore the explosive growth and investment potential within the soccer memorabilia market. As sport continues to captivate audiences worldwide, now is the time to consider adding iconic pieces to your collection.

- Women's sports memorabilia

Women's sports memorabilia is another area that's gaining traction, and not just in soccer. Historically, this sector was underdeveloped, often overlooked in favor of more established male-dominated sports markets, however as women's sports continue to gain visibility, recognition, and financial backing, memorabilia from female athletes is fast becoming a sought-after investment opportunity.

What we're seeing today isn't just a surge in women's soccer, women are making a mark across all sports. Whether it's basketball, motorsports, track and field, combat sports, or even e-sports, the distinction between male and female sports is becoming increasingly irrelevant. The barriers which once restricted female athletes to specific sports and lower visibility have begun to crumble. Opportunities and funding are becoming more equalized, and the financial rewards are following suit.

Well known athletes like Serena Williams, Simone Biles, Megan Rapinoe, and Danica Patrick have done more for women's sport than just break records; they've broken down barriers for generations to come. Serena Williams, who revolutionized tennis, and Megan Rapinoe, a trailblazer in soccer, are paving the way for younger athletes. The pioneers of women's sports, like Billie Jean King, who fought for equality in tennis and whose memorabilia has become an iconic part of history, have also played a major role. Her legacy, alongside Jackie Joyner-Kersee's achievements in athletics and Mia Hamm's dominance in women's soccer, laid the foundation for the women's sports revolution we're seeing today.

And there's a new generation of women athletes who are blazing their own trails. Naomi Osaka in tennis, Chloe Kim in snowboarding, Elena Delle Donne in basketball, and Sabrina Ionescu are just a few examples of young athletes who are already reshaping their respective sports. Their memorabilia, from signed jerseys to exclusive photos, is already attracting the attention of collectors. As their careers progress, the value of their items will only increase, making this an exciting time for those looking to invest in emerging stars.

- Golf memorabilia

Golf memorabilia has transitioned from a niche interest to a burgeoning investment sector. It encompasses a wide range of items, from signed photographs and tee markers to Ryder Cup clothing. Notably, items signed by legends such as Tony Jacklin and Nick Faldo are particularly sought after.

The golf products market is projected to reach $10.1 billion by 2030, driven by factors such as increasing participation and the rise of golf tourism in emerging markets like India and the Middle East. This growth is further fueled by the increasing number of golf courses and facilities worldwide, enhancing the sport's accessibility and appeal. A big contributor to its growth is that more women are taking up the game than ever before.

Women now represent one of the fastest-growing demographics in golf participation globally, with programs like LPGA*USGA Girls Golf seeing membership spike and major brands investing in female-focused golf gear and media. As visibility of women's golf rises, so does the potential for memorabilia from stars like Nelly Korda, Lexi Thompson, and Lydia Ko to gain collector value.

At the same time, the influx of young talent into professional golf is invigorating the sport's global profile. Players like Collin Morikawa, Viktor Hovland, and Scottie Scheffler are not only achieving success on the course but also becoming influential figures off it. Their growing popularity is reflected in the increasing demand for memorabilia associated with them.

High-quality memorabilia such as signed tournament flags, vintage clubs, and limited-edition merchandise, are becoming valuable assets. For instance, a signed 1999 PGA Championship flag by Tiger Woods sold for $4,260.75, illustrating the significant appreciation potential of such items.

- Boxing memorabilia

Boxing related items also hold substantial value in sports memorabilia. Muhammad Ali's signed pieces are especially prized, with some items bearing his signature selling for up to $14,000. Collectibles from other boxing greats like Mike Tyson and Joe Frazier also attract significant interest. Muhammad Ali's white satin trunks worn during the 1975 "Thrilla in Manila" fight against Joe Frazier, are up for auction at Sotheby's, New York, and are expected to fetch $4-6 million, and this sector is experiencing a renaissance, driven by the legacy of past champions and the rise of new stars.

The global boxing market was valued at $8.2 billion in 2025 and is projected to expand at a CAGR of 4.8%, reaching a value of $11.29 billion by 2032. This growth is fueled by the increasing popularity of combat sports, fitness trends, celebrity boxing events, and advancements in boxing equipment and training technologies.

Boxing legends are transcending the sport, becoming media stars and cultural icons. Mike Tyson's ventures into acting, Sugar Ray Leonard's television appearances, and other former champions' involvement in entertainment have broadened their appeal, attracting new fans and collectors. This crossover into mainstream media enhances the desirability for memorabilia associated with these athletes.

- Athletics memorabilia

Track and field have broad global reach, with events like the Olympics and the World Championships regularly capturing the attention of millions. Notably, items tied to historic performances from the 2012 London Olympics have significantly bolstered the value of athletics memorabilia.

The London Games were a landmark event for British athletics, with stars like Jessica Ennis-Hill, Mo Farah, and Greg Rutherford achieving iconic feats that have left a lasting impression on fans and collectors. Jessica Ennis-Hill's gold medal-winning performance in the heptathlon and Mo Farah's dominant victories in the 5000m and 10,000m are unforgettable moments in Olympic history, and memorabilia tied to these athletes, whether it's signed race bibs, official merchandise, or medals, continues to rise in demand.

While the Summer Olympics often dominate the spotlight in track and field, the Winter Olympics also provide unique opportunities for collectors. With iconic events such as skiing, snowboarding, figure skating, and ice hockey, winter athletes are just as revered, and their memorabilia can be equally prized. Collectibles tied to figures like Shaun White,

Lindsey Vonn, and Tessa Virtue have begun to gain significant traction, Shaun White's signed snowboard or Lindsey Vonn's race-worn skis are items that not only hold great sentimental value but are rapidly becoming sought-after collector's items. As the Winter Olympics continue to grow in popularity, memorabilia linked to such athletes, their achievements, and their iconic moments are expected to increase in value.

In the same breath, the Paralympic Games, which celebrate the incredible achievements of athletes with disabilities, have also become a rising force in the memorabilia market. These athletes represent incredible perseverance, dedication, and triumph over adversity, and the Paralympic Games provide a platform for their stories to be told. As these events gain in stature, the memorabilia that comes from the athletes involved will continue to rise in value.

Handicapped athletes like Tanni Grey-Thompson- who became one of the most successful Paralympic athletes in history- have already seen the value of their memorabilia increase as collectors recognize the significance of their performances. After achieving 11 gold medals across five games, her signed racing gloves from the Sydney Paralympics sold for over £4000 at auction, and her personal racing chair went for a cool £7,500. The inclusion of athletes from all backgrounds in the Paralympic Games also raises the interest in this unique segment of the sports memorabilia world. For example, memorabilia from iconic performances, like David Weir's dominance in wheelchair racing or Ellie Simmonds' exceptional career in swimming, holds tremendous potential for collectors looking to secure items from those athletes whose performances have transcended the traditional boundaries of sport. Simmonds, who won her first gold medal at just 13, has seen a surge in interest for her memorabilia, with a signed swimming hat and goggles from Beijing 2008 appraised at £2000.

- Formula 1

Formula 1 is experiencing an unprecedented surge in popularity, transforming from a niche motorsport into a global entertainment powerhouse. In 2024, F1's global fanbase soared to 826.5 million, marking a 12% increase from the previous year. This growth is driven by significant gains in markets such as China, Canada, Argentina, Saudi Arabia, and the United States.

The United States in particular has become a focal point for F1's expansion. With three races now on the calendar - Miami, Austin, and Las Vegas - American viewership has seen a substantial rise. The inaugural Las Vegas Grand Prix in 2023 attracted an average audience of 1.3 million, despite its late-night start time. The Netflix series *Drive to Survive* has played a pivotal role in this surge, with 25% of viewers reporting they became fans after watching the show.

At the same time, new teams and circuits are adding to the sport's allure. The addition of races in cities like Las Vegas and the potential for future events in Thailand and other global locations are expanding F1's reach and appeal.

Emerging drivers are also capturing the public's imagination. Oscar Piastri's victory at the Chinese Grand Prix in 2025 has positioned him as a rising star, while Lando Norris continues to be a fan favorite. Their performances are not only elevating McLaren's profile but also increasing demand for memorabilia associated with these drivers.

It will come as no surprise that as F1's popularity grows, so does the value of its memorabilia. Items associated with legendary figures like Ayrton Senna and Michael Schumacher have long been coveted by collectors. More recently, memorabilia from current stars such as Lewis Hamilton and Max Verstappen are commanding impressive prices- in 2022, a 2006 Lewis Hamilton rookie card sold for a record $312,000 (*Plate 2.5*), setting a new benchmark for F1 collectibles.

Platforms like F1 Authentics and RM Sotheby's are facilitating the sale of rare and valuable items, including race-worn helmets, signed gloves, and limited-edition merchandise. These auctions are attracting a global audience, with bidders from Europe, the Middle East, and the Americas, vying for exclusive F1 memorabilia.

- Cricket

Cricket's global viewership exceeds 2.5 billion people, and memorabilia from iconic players like Sachin Tendulkar and Virat Kohli are likely to become highly sought after. Cricket's expanding presence in markets like the U.S. and Asia, combined with the growing Indian Premier League (IPL), presents a promising avenue for memorabilia collectors.

The collectibles market in India is projected to reach approximately $22.75 billion by 2030, growing at a CAGR of 7% from 2025 to 2030. Within this, trading cards are the fastest-growing segment, indicating a surge in interest in collectible items like cricket memorabilia.

The IPL, established in 2008, has become a significant force in the sport, with a brand value estimated at $12 billion in 2024. The league's media rights for the 2023–2027 period were sold for $6.4 billion, reflecting its massive commercial appeal. This growth has spurred a surge in demand for memorabilia associated with IPL teams and players.

Notably, cricket memorabilia auctions have seen impressive sales. MS Dhoni's bat from the 2011 World Cup final sold for INR 83 lakhs (around $44,000), while a bat signed by the Indian team fetched INR 6 lakh (around $7000) at an auction supporting the Indian Head Injury Foundation. These sales underscore the increasing value placed on cricket memorabilia in India.

Bollywood stars are also entering the cricket memorabilia scene. For instance, KL Rahul and Athiya Shetty organized an auction where jerseys worn by players like Virat Kohli and MS Dhoni were sold to support charitable causes. Such involvement from high-profile figures is expected to further elevate the status and value of cricket memorabilia in India.

As the IPL continues to attract international talent and the sport's popularity grows, the market for cricket memorabilia in India is set to expand, offering lucrative opportunities for collectors and investors alike.

* * *

The sports memorabilia industry is undergoing a major transformation, driven by the entry and evolution of key players who are helping to establish a more formalized and expansive marketplace. Companies like Fanatics have emerged as dominant forces, leveraging massive financial backing to reshape how memorabilia is distributed, graded, and authenticated. Alongside online breaks and auction platforms like Whatnot, Loop, and eBay Live, collectors can buy into real-time card breaks, creating a gamified, fast-paced collecting experience that appeals to both seasoned investors and younger, tech-savvy fans. These formats not only democratize access but also create constant market liquidity.

Card companies themselves have adapted to demand by launching high-end product lines that prioritize scarcity and exclusivity. Brands like Panini have created premium categories such as National Treasures, Immaculate, Flawless, and Noir, each with limited print runs and luxury-level packaging. These sets often feature on-card autographs, game-used materials, and ultra-short print (USP) inserts. Moreover, serial-numbered cards like 1/1, 1/5, 1/10, and /25- have become the centerpiece of modern collecting, driving up demand and secondary market prices as collectors chase the rarest possible variants.

The influence of these companies extends across trading cards, digital platforms, and even ownership models. Fanatics is the Amazon of sports collectibles right now. Backed by billions, they've locked down exclusive deals with major sports leagues like the NFL, NBA, MLB, and even global entities like UEFA and FIFA. They've streamlined the entire supply chain - from athlete signings to authentication to fulfillment - under one roof. Fanatics Collectibles is now the main distributor of Topps trading cards, and with that move, they effectively took over the most iconic baseball card brand in history.

Alongside Fanatics, industry staples such as PSA, Beckett, and Goldin Auctions continue to play pivotal roles in setting standards for authentication and valuation. Goldin Auctions, for example, leads when it comes to high-end sports memorabilia. They've set world records on items from Jordan, Ruth, Mantle, and Ali. They operate like an art auction house, only their "paintings" are cleats, jerseys, and cards with historical gravity. Meanwhile, online auction platforms and social media are opening new channels for discovery and engagement, further fueling interest and access. Innovations like blockchain-based authentication and fractional ownership are helping to create a more transparent, scalable, and investable market. Together, these developments are not just increasing the size of the market, they're establishing the infrastructure, protocol, and trust necessary to support its future growth.

Conventions are also driving growth. The in-person sports collectibles convention scene is exploding. We're talking:

- The National Sports Collectors Convention (NSCC) (July - August) - Think of it like the Super Bowl for collectors. Every major dealer, buyer, athlete, and investor shows up. Live deals. Breakout panels. Private high-end trades behind velvet curtains.

- Fanatics Fest (debuted in 2024) (June) - Combines athletes, pop culture, entertainment, and card breaks. It's Coachella meets collectibles.

- Regional shows in places like Chicago, Dallas, and Miami are also gaining momentum, fueled by younger collectors and TikTok-era exposure.

Why does this matter? Because community builds trust, and trust drives value. These conventions aren't just social events, they're marketplaces with real economic impact.

With the continued influx of capital, technology, and expertise, the sports memorabilia sector is poised for even greater growth and excitement in the coming years. To illustrate the value this market can command, Table 2 highlights four of the most expensive sports memorabilia items ever sold. These extraordinary figures underscore not only the emotional and cultural weight attached to these items, but also their rising legitimacy as alternative investment assets. Appendix 7 provides a list of the top 10 items for further review:

Table 2: Most Expensive Sports Memorabilia of All Time

ITEM	SPORT	PRICE (USD)	SALE YEAR	ADDITIONAL INFORMATION
Babe Ruth's 1932 "Called Shot" Jersey	Baseball	$24.12M	2024	Worn during Ruth's legendary "called shot" in the 1932 World Series. Sold at Heritage Auctions.

1952 Topps Mickey Mantle Baseball Card	Baseball	$12.6M	2022	Mint+ 9.5 graded card. One of the rarest and most iconic cards in sports history.
Michael Jordan's 1998 NBA Finals Jersey	Basketball (NBA)	$10.1M	2022	Worn in Game 1 of his last Finals with the Bulls. Sold at Sotheby's.
Diego Maradona's 1986 "Hand of God" Shirt	Soccer (Football)	$9.28M	2022	Worn during the infamous quarterfinal vs. England. Auctioned by former player Steve Hodge.

Source: Heritage Auctions, Sotheby's, and Time Magazine, 2019–2024

Note: *For a full list of the top 10 highest-selling sports memorabilia items, refer to Appendix 7.*

Entertainment Memorabilia

If you've ever wished you could own a piece of your favorite movie, TV show, or musical performance, collecting entertainment memorabilia might just be your perfect entry into the world of collectibles. Imagine owning something as iconic as Dorothy's ruby slippers from *The Wizard of Oz*, or a signed script from *Friends*. Dorothy's iconic ruby slippers *(Plate 2.6)* were auctioned off in 2015 at Heritage auction for an astounding $32 million. As a piece of cinematic history, they've been sought after for decades, but their value skyrocketed when they changed hands at a major auction. The slippers were sold by a private collector who had acquired them years earlier, and their sale helped elevate the concept of *film memorabilia* to a whole new level.

Entertainment memorabilia encompass a wide range of items related to movies, TV shows, theater, and music. They include:

- Scripts – For example, a signed script of Star Wars: A New Hope, or a copy of Friends' pilot script.

- Costumes - Such as Dorothy's ruby slippers from The Wizard of Oz, or a Batman costume worn by Michael Keaton in Batman (1989).

- Props - Like the DeLorean from Back to the Future, or the ring worn by Frodo in The Lord of the Rings trilogy.

- Trading cards - Rare and graded entertainment trading cards such as the original *Star Wars* Topps cards, *Pokémon* 1st Edition cards, or vintage *Marvel Universe* sets.

The famous jacket worn by Marlon Brando in *The Godfather*- the one he donned as Vito Corleone, the head of the infamous Corleone family- sold at a Sotheby's auction for $1.02 million in 2016. This jacket had been sitting in a private collection for decades, but when it was finally sold, it connected the buyer not only to the world of *The Godfather* but to the very essence of Hollywood's golden age. The sale made headlines and forever changed the collector's life, as they now own a tangible piece of one of cinema's most legendary roles.

The global entertainment memorabilia market is valued at approximately $10 billion in 2025 and is projected to grow at a 6.5% CAGR from 2025 to 2030. This growth is fueled by a resurgence in nostalgia, the influence of streaming platforms, and an increasing demand for items linked to beloved franchises and historical entertainment moments. As fanbases continue to expand and media consumption evolves, the market for entertainment memorabilia presents substantial opportunities for collectors at all levels.

For example, in 2021, a script from *Breaking Bad*- the unforgettable episode titled "Ozymandias"- sold for a staggering $36,000 at Bonhams auction house. This wasn't just any script, though. Signed by the creator Vince Gilligan and the show's stars, Bryan Cranston, Aaron Paul, and Anna Gunn, it was a coveted piece of TV history. The emotional weight of the episode, which marked a pivotal moment in the show's plot, combined with the celebrity signatures, made this script a highly desirable item, and the sale was a dream come true for its new owner.

Entertainment memorabilia are becoming one of the most emotionally resonant and financially promising sectors in the collectible landscape. As new platforms emerge and audiences evolve, several key trends are shaping the future of this market.

First, the concept of "nostalgia economics" is gaining traction. Millennials and Gen Xers who grew up with franchises like *Harry Potter*, *Star Wars*, *Disney*, and *Friends*, now possess greater disposable income. Their desire to reconnect with beloved childhood and teen memories is driving massive demand for items from the 80s, 90s, and early 2000s. The emotional weight of these memories is increasingly matched by real market value. Not only that, but streaming platforms are breathing new life into legacy franchises. Shows like *Cobra Kai*, *The Mandalorian*, *Stranger Things*, and *Beckham* have sparked renewed interest in vintage props, toys, posters, and costumes associated with earlier eras. The ability to rediscover and binge past content fuels collector enthusiasm across generations.

Like sports memorabilia, entertainment memorabilia are emerging as an alternative investment class. Auction houses are beginning to treat these items with the same prestige once reserved for fine art and rare books. They are listed alongside paintings and sculpture, valued not just for their nostalgia but for their strong appreciation potential. Entertainment memorabilia are moving from the margins of elite collecting into the mainstream of cultural and financial relevance. As the barriers to access lower and technology deepens trust, fans, investors, and collectors alike are finding new reasons to engage. From museum-worthy artifacts to fan-driven sales on social media, the sector's appeal is as diverse as the stories it helps preserve.

Here are some of the highest selling entertainment memorabilia so far. The top four are presented below for context, while a complete list of the top ten can be found in Appendix 7.

Table 3: Most Expensive Entertainment Memorabilia of All Time

ITEM	CATEGORY	PRICE (USD)	YEAR OF SALE	ADDITIONAL INFORMATION
Dorothy's Ruby Slippers	Movie Prop (The Wizard of Oz)	$32 million	2015	Worn by Judy Garland in *The Wizard of Oz*. Sold at Heritage Auctions.
Marilyn Monroe's "Happy Birthday" Dress	Movie Costume (Hollywood)	$4.8 million	2016	Worn by Monroe during her famous 1962 performance for President John F. Kennedy's birthday celebration. Sold at Julien's Auctions.

The Batmobile (1966)	Movie Prop (Batman) *(Plate 2.7)*	$4.62 million	2013	The original Batmobile used in the 1966 Batman TV series sold at Barrett-Jackson.
The DeLorean from Back to the Future	Movie Prop (Back to the Future)	$4.1 million	2022	Auctioned by Barrett-Jackson.

Source: Compiled from Heritage Auctions, Julien's Auctions, Barrett-Jackson, Bonhams, and Christie's, 2013–2023.

Note: *For a full list of the top 10 highest-selling entertainment memorabilia items, refer to Appendix 7.*

Opportunities in the Market

The entertainment memorabilia market is evolving rapidly, driven by the growing demand for iconic items across films, television shows and music. As entertainment continues to shape pop culture, opportunities for both seasoned collectors and newcomers have never been greater. Here's a closer look at what is established, what is growing rapidly, and what remains untapped in this dynamic market.

- Iconic movie memorabilia

Certain sectors of the entertainment memorabilia market are firmly established, with consistent demand from collectors and fans alike. Movie memorabilia, particularly from iconic films and franchises, has always commanded high prices. Items from *Star Wars*, *The Wizard of Oz*, *The Godfather*, and *James Bond* continue to set records at auction houses.

The emergence of China and India as prominent centers for film production and entertainment has significantly expanded the global market for this type of memorabilia. China's film industry has experienced remarkable growth, with projections indicating that by 2027, it will surpass the United States in box office revenue, accounting for

27% of the global market share. This expansion is fueled by substantial investments from both domestic and international companies such as Alibaba and Tencent, which have enhanced production capabilities and distribution networks. Additionally, China's burgeoning fan economy, valued at approximately CNY 4.942 trillion in 2021 (around $682 million), has bolstered demand for celebrity-endorsed products, including memorabilia.

Similarly, India's film industry- particularly Bollywood- has garnered international acclaim, with films like *Dangal* achieving significant success in foreign markets. The Indian collectibles market is projected to reach $22.7 billion by 2030, growing at a CAGR of 7%. This growth is driven by a rising middle class and increased disposable income, leading to greater interest in collecting entertainment memorabilia. Together, China and India represent a dynamic and expanding sector in the entertainment memorabilia market, offering new opportunities for collectors and investors seeking to diversify their portfolios with culturally significant items.

Limited edition items also attract attention from all corners. As film studios increasingly produce limited-edition or special release items, there is untapped potential in collectibles related to these releases. For example, limited-edition movie posters, specially designed props, or unique, one-of-a-kind production materials are starting to catch the eye of collectors.

- Television memorabilia

The demand for TV-related memorabilia has grown significantly, particularly for items from beloved shows like *Friends*, *I Love Lucy* and *Breaking Bad*. In 2021, a signed script from *Breaking Bad*'s iconic episode "Ozymandias" sold for $36,000 at Bonhams auction, highlighting the rising value of television memorabilia. As streaming platforms like Netflix,

Disney+, and Hulu continue to dominate the entertainment landscape, there is a growing demand for memorabilia from modern shows which have achieved cult followings. Series like *Stranger Things* have driven demand by tapping into '80s nostalgia from vintage-inspired costumes to collectible props, while newer titles such as *The Penguin* (from the *Batman* universe) and top-ranked streaming hits frequently spark fresh waves of interest. As these shows build massive fan bases and cultural footprints, their memorabilia are becoming highly sought-after collectibles, reflecting both fandom and long-term value. Stranger Things reignited a love for all things 80s, with a signed retro bike from the show reaching nearly $8000 at an auction in 2023.

The demand is especially high for signed scripts, costumes, and props from popular series. Nostalgic items, like a prop from *Friends* or *The Office*, are increasingly fetching high prices at auctions, as a younger generation of collectors enters the market; the infamous orange couch from Central Perk in Friends sold for $14,500 at a charity auction. As streaming content becomes more pervasive, the market for TV-related collectibles is expected to grow even faster, especially with shows from the '80s and '90s gaining renewed attention.

The U.S. remains the biggest market for entertainment memorabilia, driven by the massive Hollywood legacy and the longstanding popularity of American TV shows and films. The country's auction houses routinely set records for high-value sales; in 2021 alone, Christie's auctioned off memorabilia from *Star Wars*, *The Godfather*, and *James Bond*, contributing to the U.S.'s dominant position in the market. The European market is also strong, particularly in the UK and France, where auction houses like Bonhams and Drouot have consistently seen high demand for memorabilia from historical film franchises and iconic cultural moments. Specifically, the UK has seen significant growth in *Harry*

Potter and *James Bond* collectibles. Letters and wands from Harry Potter have sold for anything from £10,000 to £30,000 in UK based auctions,

So, whether you're dreaming of owning a script signed by the cast of *Friends* or a vintage prop from *The Godfather*, now is the perfect time to start collecting. And there are still untapped areas with significant growth potential in the entertainment memorabilia space. As the market for traditional items expands, these emerging sectors present new opportunities for collectors.

- Soundtrack memorabilia

While film memorabilia primarily revolve around visual items like props and costumes, the market for music-related memorabilia is a growing segment. Soundtracks, original film scores, and rare music-related pieces from films and TV shows are becoming increasingly sought after. Items such as signed soundtracks or limited-edition vinyl records from iconic films are likely to appreciate significantly in value. In 2021, a fully orchestrated, annotated score sheet for *Star Wars*, by John Williams, sold for £18,75- at Bonhams, while *Stranger Things* retro 80's soundtrack has sparked a love of 80's music and vinyl, with limited edition 'Upside Down' red vinyl sets signed by the composers, regularly selling for between £500 and £1200.

- Digital creator and YouTube memorabilia

One of the most untapped and rapidly emerging sectors in entertainment memorabilia lies within the world of digital creators. Platforms like YouTube, TikTok, and Twitch have cultivated global fan bases rivaling those of traditional celebrities, yet their memorabilia market remains in its infancy. High-profile creators such as MrBeast and Charli D'Amelio command tens of millions of followers and have begun to influence merchandise and content culture at scale.

Signed merchandise, limited-edition drops, original video props, and exclusive content-related items are increasingly viewed as collector-worthy. As these creators continue to build brand empires and transition into mainstream entertainment, demand for their early memorabilia is expected to rise dramatically.

A new trend in the entertainment memorabilia market is the role of virality in boosting item value. Content creators and fan communities now drive visibility through platforms like Instagram, TikTok, and YouTube, where rare collectibles are showcased, unboxed, and reviewed. The social currency of owning a unique or signed item often translates directly into resale value. As more collectors share and promote their pieces, and creators spotlight memorabilia in their content, value is increasingly tied to cultural relevance and digital exposure.

- Music icons and signed albums

Music memorabilia beyond soundtracks-especially signed albums and personal items- remains a relatively untapped market. Artists like Taylor Swift, Beyoncé, The Weekend, and Billie Eilish have huge global audiences with deep emotional connections to their music. Swift in particular has leaned into collector culture, releasing limited vinyl editions and signed albums that now resell at significant markups. As music fandom increasingly intersects with digital platforms and behind-the-scenes content, we're likely to see rising demand for memorabilia like tour-used instruments, handwritten lyrics, and personalized collectibles.

Driving this market are some of the most prestigious auction houses in the world; Heritage Auctions has cemented its reputation as a dominant force in entertainment memorabilia and in 2024 alone, they recorded a record-breaking $38.6 million in sales in this category. That total was powered in part by the historic $32.5 million sale of Dorothy's ruby slippers from *The Wizard of Oz*, an auction that shook the industry and helped redefine how we value cinematic history. Heritage operates globally, with strong footholds in Dallas, New York, and Hong Kong, and they've built a serious reputation for commanding the spotlight when rare Hollywood items hit the block.

Sotheby's, of course, remains a juggernaut. With global sales reaching $7.9 billion across all categories in 2023, their entertainment division is no afterthought. Sotheby's has handled headline-making pieces like Jimi Hendrix's Woodstock guitar, which sold for $2 million in 2020. This was a landmark moment, not just for music memorabilia but for the broader understanding of how cultural legacy translates into tangible, investable value. Their global presence across New York, London, and Hong Kong allows them to tap into elite buyers from every corner of the globe.

Christie's, too, is deeply entrenched in the world of entertainment collectibles. They recorded around $6.2 billion in global sales in 2023, and handled numerous high-value sales, including the $1.02 million sale of Marlon Brando's *Godfather* jacket. Christie's has a legacy of pushing the envelope in film and fashion memorabilia, and their entertainment auctions have steadily grown in influence and value. They remain a go-to for elite collectors seeking authenticity, exclusivity, and historical significance.

Bonhams, while a bit more niche, has made a name for itself in the realm of cinematic and cultural memorabilia. Known for more specialized offerings, Bonhams continues to attract collectors of specific franchises including *Star Wars*, *Breakfast at Tiffany's*, and *The Godfather*. Their auctions in London and Los Angeles cater to a more curated clientele, and they consistently deliver in categories that combine nostalgia with craftsmanship.

In any collectibles market, authenticity is the foundation of value, and the entertainment space is no exception. The most trusted names in verification include PSA/DNA, which has long set the bar for autograph and memorabilia authentication. Their role in establishing legitimacy and preserving trust can't be overstated. Similarly, JSA (James Spence Authentication) is highly regarded, particularly in the TV and music memorabilia spaces, and Beckett Authentication Services- well-known for its authority in sports- has expanded effectively into entertainment autographs and pop culture pieces. These authenticators are gatekeepers, ensuring the integrity of this booming market.

But perhaps what's driving the most visible momentum today are the conventions and collector expos that bring these communities together and spark the thrill of the hunt in person.

1. Collect-A-Con

   2025 Tour Dates:

   • Houston, TX: April 26–27
   • Orlando, FL: June 7–8
   • Chicago, IL: August 16–17
   • Denver, CO: October 4–5
   • Miami, FL: November 22–23

Features over 500 dealers, celebrity guests, and live concerts, focusing on trading cards, comics, and vintage toys.

2. WonderCon 2025

   Dates: March 28–30, 2025 in Anaheim Convention Center, Anaheim, CA

   Offers exclusive panels, creator meet-and-greets, and a vibrant exhibit hall celebrating comics and pop culture.

3. CT HorrorFest 2025

   Dates: Stamford, CT: May 3–4, Hartford, CT: September 20–21

   Brings together horror fans with celebrity guests, panels, and a variety of vendors, offering unique horror memorabilia.

Historical and Political Memorabilia

Imagine holding a letter once penned by Abraham Lincoln himself, or owning a piece of the Berlin Wall, real artifacts that have witnessed history unfold. These are the things that make up historical and political memorabilia. The connection to monumental events and figures adds an emotional and financial value unlike any other. These items come in many forms, from documents and artifacts to campaign materials, each with their own story to tell. They include:

- Documents – Think of a signed letter by George Washington or a first edition of the U.S. Constitution.
- Artifacts – Pieces of history like a shard from the Berlin Wall, a WWII soldier's medal or hair from a former president, can become priceless treasures.
- Campaign materials – Collectibles like John F. Kennedy's 1960 campaign button or a signed photograph of Winston Churchill evoke the political movements that shaped nations.
- Dinosaur bones - These have been getting a lot of attention after scientific breakthroughs and movies like Jurassic Park, which bring them to the general public.
- Royal memorabilia - Items associated with the British royal family and other monarchies, such as Queen Victoria's mourning jewelry, coronation programs,

or Princess Diana's handwritten letters, are deeply sought after.

- Coins and stamps

Each piece is valuable not only because of its rarity but because it connects you to a key moment in history, allowing you to hold a tangible connection to the past. Documents tied to events like the American Revolution, Civil War, or World War II can fetch significant sums, especially when they are linked to iconic historical figures or moments.

As of 2025, the historical and political memorabilia market is valued at approximately $6 billion, and it is expected to grow at a CAGR of 5-6% from 2025 to 2030.

Interest in historical and political memorabilia is expanding globally. In Africa, post-colonial archives and artifacts from liberation movements are drawing collectors. In Asia, items from the Mao era, Indian independence, and the Meiji period of Japan are rising in value. Middle Eastern demand is focused on Ottoman-era documents, Gulf royal artifacts, and memorabilia linked to the post-oil transitions of the 20th century. Latin America sees strong interest in figures like Che Guevara and Simón Bolívar, while in the Western world, tech-authenticated World War relics and Cold War-era items remain mainstays alongside a growing market for royal memorabilia tied to the British crown.

Historical and political memorabilia are cultural touchstones. They speak to power and memory in ways few other objects can and are deeply tied to cultural and national identity. They don't just represent the past, they define it. For many nations, key artifacts form part of a shared memory, and their possession can reflect political influence or cultural pride. As a result, it's not uncommon for museums, governments, and academic institutions to compete fiercely with private buyers at auctions. These aren't just purchases, they're acts of historical stewardship.

Their value is also driven by permanent scarcity. Unlike comic books or sports cards, historical artifacts aren't mass-produced. There will never be another letter handwritten by a Civil War general, or another campaign button actually worn in 1960. These items are one-of-a-kind, tied to moments that can never be replicated. Once they're gone - or locked in a collection or museum - they may never come to the market again.

That is why provenance is everything. The story behind the item often determines its price. A signed letter from Winston Churchill is valuable on its own, but one dated just before D-Day, with documentation of its journey through time, can be priceless. The Buyer Pool is unique as well. This market attracts high-income individuals, legacy-minded collectors, foundations, and even national governments, often driven by a desire to preserve national history or cement institutional credibility. In many cases, the buyer is investing not just in an object, but in a long-term narrative.

Geopolitical shifts also shape demand. When tensions rise, so does interest in the material culture of conflict. Soviet-era items and Cold War relics have surged in value as global anxieties rekindle interest in past struggles. Similarly, Chinese revolutionary artifacts or memorabilia tied to anti-colonial movements are becoming more sought-after, especially by buyers in emerging markets who see these items as powerful symbols of identity and resistance.

At the same time, the digital history market is beginning to take shape. AI can now recreate lost or damaged documents, while NFTs are being used to link digital versions of artifacts with verified provenance. Virtual museums, immersive archives, and AI-narrated exhibits are transforming how people interact with history and offering new ways to preserve and share stories that were once only accessible in physical form.

What was once the domain of scholars and elite collectors is rapidly becoming a global, tech-integrated marketplace. Political and historical memorabilia are evolving, bridging the past with the future and expanding the very definition of what it means to own a piece of history.

Opportunities in the Market

The historical and political memorabilia market is a thriving space with established areas of high value and emerging opportunities.

- U.S presidents & politics memorabilia

Items related to the U.S. Presidents and political figures consistently dominate this market. Memorabilia like signed letters, inaugural items, and significant speeches have been the bread and butter for collectors for decades. Documents connected to figures like George Washington, Abraham Lincoln, and John F. Kennedy are always in high demand, with certain pieces fetching millions. Presidential campaign buttons, like those from Kennedy's 1960 run, remain valuable, often reaching prices of $20,000 or more at auctions. A first-edition copy of the U.S. Constitution sold for an astounding $43.2 million in 2021, marking the highest price ever paid for a document at auction.

- World-war memorabilia

Historical artifacts tied to monumental events like World War I and World War II are extremely collectible, with items such as military uniforms, medals, and pilot helmets frequently appearing at auctions. A WWII soldier's medal or a vintage pilot's helmet can easily fetch tens of thousands of dollars, depending on its rarity and historical significance. Medals awarded to famous soldiers or related to historic battles are especially desirable.

Other, previously untapped categories, are growing too:

- Non-American political memorabilia

While U.S. political items are well-established, non-American political memorabilia has not reached the same level of demand, but is growing. Campaign materials and artifacts related to political leaders from non-Western countries, such as Africa, Asia, or South America, are still emerging in the marketplace. But as global political narratives continue to intertwine, there's potential for a surge in value. Mandela memorabilia, for instance, is gaining traction.

- Grassroots movement memorabilia

Another exciting area to watch is memorabilia from grassroots movements and protests, such as the Civil Rights Movement and environmental protests. These items are still in the early stages of development as collectible markets, but with history continually evolving, they may become highly sought-after in the future.

- Icons and infamy

Another powerful yet often controversial area of historical collecting is memorabilia tied to polarizing public figures, and criminal or political events that have shaped public discourse. Items associated with highly visible figures like Donald Trump, for instance, have begun to generate a collector's market of their own. From signed books and campaign rally materials to impeachment-related documents and trial memorabilia, collectors are already eyeing these artifacts as part of a living, unfolding historical narrative. Regardless of political stance, the sheer visibility and global impact of figures like Trump make items associated with them historically potent and culturally significant.

Similarly, there is growing interest in memorabilia related to scandals, criminal trials, and major legal or cultural flashpoints, from Watergate documents to O.J. Simpson trial artifacts. These items often generate media buzz when they hit the auction block, not just because of their historical relevance but because of their power to provoke emotion and debate. As long as society continues to be fascinated by the characters and conflicts that define eras, this "infamous memorabilia" category is likely to expand.

You don't need to be a billionaire to start collecting historical memorabilia. Many collectible items, like campaign buttons, medals, and smaller documents, are still accessible. Websites like Heritage Auctions and Bonhams regularly feature accessible historical lots that start in the $1,000 to $10,000 range, giving anyone a chance to own a piece of history. Keep an eye on auctions and estate sales in your area, as they can be great opportunities to pick up valuable pieces at lower prices. The market is booming, and there's no better time to start your own collection.

Noted below are the four most expensive historical & political memorabilia sold yet. The complete list of the top ten most expensive items can be found in Appendix 7.

Table 4: Most Expensive Historical & Political Memorabilia of All Time

ITEM	TYPE	PRICE	YEAR OF SALE	ADDITIONAL INFO
U.S. Constitution (First Edition)	Document	$43.2 million	2021	One of only 13 surviving original copies. Sold at Sotheby's to cryptocurrency entrepreneur Kurt D. Peterson.

Abraham Lincoln's Signed 1863 Emancipation Proclamation	Document	$3.7 million	2012	A historic 1863 copy signed by Lincoln himself. Sold at Sotheby's.
George Washington's Signed Letter *(Plate 2.8)*	Document	$3.4 million	2018	A letter signed by the first U.S. president. Sold at Sotheby's.
Berlin Wall Fragments	Artifact	$1.5 million	2015	Pieces of the Berlin Wall, symbolizing the end of the Cold War. Sold at Bonhams.

Sources: Sotheby's Auction Archives, Bonhams Auction Results, Heritage Auctions, RR Auction.

Note: *For a full list of the top 10 highest-selling historical & political memorabilia items, refer to Appendix 7.*

Sotheby's and Christie's are two of the most prestigious auction houses handling some of the most sought-after pieces of historical and political memorabilia. Sotheby's, for example, facilitated the sale of the First Edition U.S. Constitution for a record-breaking $43.2 million in 2021. Bonhams, RR Auction, and Heritage Auctions also play crucial roles in bringing high-value memorabilia to market, particularly presidential and political memorabilia. For instance, Heritage Auctions handled the sale of Abraham Lincoln's Blood-Stained Gloves, which sold for $68,000.

Major collectors, both private and public, also influence the market. For example, Kurt D. Peterson, the cryptocurrency entrepreneur, made headlines with his purchase of the First Edition U.S. Constitution. David Holmes, the stuntman from the Harry Potter films, brought personal historical memorabilia into the spotlight, raising the profile of items tied to significant figures in modern history. The sale of his Marauder's Map at auction fetched $299,250, highlighting the growing market for memorabilia tied to living history.

The demand for historical and political memorabilia is driven by a combination of high-profile auctions, anniversary events, and cultural shifts. Several key conventions, shows, and events contribute to the ever-growing interest in these rare items. The Propstore Auction and similar events held by Heritage Auctions and Bonhams regularly feature pieces that fetch millions. These auctions have become important cultural touchstones for collectors and investors alike. Every year, these events draw attention to rare political memorabilia like campaign buttons, inaugural tickets, and documents from iconic leaders. Auction houses have also capitalized on anniversaries and milestone events to drive interest in relevant memorabilia. For example, the centennial celebrations of World War I and the Civil Rights Movement have sparked a rise in demand for related artifacts like medals, campaign materials, and historical documents.

Events like The New York Antiquarian Book Fair, The National WWII Museum's Annual Symposium, and Comic-Con (for political and historical content) provide platforms for both established collectors and newcomers to acquire historical and political memorabilia. These events often feature special exhibits which showcase high-value historical documents, campaign materials, and rare artifacts. For example, the National Archives and Smithsonian Institution routinely host exhibitions showcasing significant historical documents and artifacts that are frequently reproduced in limited quantities for collectors to purchase. These limited-edition pieces often skyrocket in value.

Finally, the political climate- especially during presidential elections- provides ample opportunity for the sale and purchase of memorabilia. Political memorabilia tied to the 2020 U.S. Presidential Election, such as campaign materials, official ballots, and rally merchandise, was widely collected and traded. As the cultural significance of events like impeachments, military campaigns, or historical trials rises, memorabilia related to these periods (such as trial documents or campaign materials) gains value.

Pop Culture Memorabilia

Imagine owning the original action figure of Darth Vader, still in its packaging, or holding the first ever Superman comic; pieces of pop culture history that connect you directly to the films, TV shows, and games you've loved for decades. Pop culture memorabilia often focus on collectibles from movies, TV shows, comic books, and video games which have gained a cult following or mainstream appeal.

The pop culture memorabilia market is valued at $4–5 billion, with an expected CAGR of 8-9% from 2025 to 2030, making it one of the fastest-growing sectors in the collectibles world.

Unlike general entertainment memorabilia, pop culture memorabilia specifically revolves around the products and characters that form the foundation of modern entertainment and fandom. These items are often tied to massive franchises and can stir deep nostalgia for the fans who grew up with them. They include things like:

- Toys – Items like vintage Star Wars action figures, a 1950s Barbie doll, or a first-edition GI Joe action figure can hold immense value, especially if still in their original packaging.
- Comics – Consider Action Comics #1, which introduced Superman, or a first edition of The Amazing Spider-Man #1. These iconic comic books have driven the market for decades.

- Merchandise – Think limited-edition Harry Potter wands, a Funko Pop figure from Stranger Things, or a Star Wars Stormtrooper helmet. Items tied to cult favorites often see surges in value with every new installment or anniversary.

- Video games – Items such as sealed, mint condition copies of early games, rare game cartridges, original game maps and signed collector's copies. Even game related merch and add-ons; a limited run of Halo 2 Master Chief Helmets (2004) signed by Bungie developers are individually worth between $2500 and $5000.

The beauty of pop culture memorabilia is that it appeals to nostalgia, representing the stories, characters, and franchises that have shaped popular culture over the years. Blockbuster films, comic book universes, and video game franchises are constantly growing, meaning the market has huge potential for both fans and collectors looking to invest.

Many collectors have flipped their passion into profit through pop culture memorabilia and changed their lives forever. In 2017, a rare collection of 12 original Star Wars action figures (released in 1977 by Kenner) sold for an incredible $27,000 at Hake's auctions. The set- which included beloved characters like Luke Skywalker, Princess Leia, and Han Solo- was worth so much because it was still in near-mint condition, with many figures in their original packaging, something extremely rare for Star Wars toys from that era. The collection was sold at auction by a private seller who had inherited it, and the buyer, a passionate collector, added the set to his home museum.

In a similar story, a sealed copy of the original Super Mario Bros. game for the Nintendo Entertainment System (NES) sold for a mind-blowing $2 million in 2021 at Heritage auctions. This game is considered a cornerstone of video game history and was graded 9.8 A+ by Wata Games, marking it as a perfect example of retro gaming. The game was originally purchased by a collector who had carefully preserved it since the late 1980s, and the sale made waves, demonstrating just how coveted these vintage video game items can be. In fact, this record-breaking sale increased the appeal of video game memorabilia, a market that is still relatively young but rapidly growing.

Opportunities in the Market

The pop culture memorabilia market is booming, but it varies in value depending on the type of item and its connection to the fandom it belongs to.

- Comics

The comic book market is deeply established. Action Comics #1, where Superman first appeared, was sold for $3.2 million in 2014 at Metropolis collectibles, setting the bar for comic book values. Comic books featuring first appearances of characters like Spider-Man, Iron Man, or Batman are always in demand, with some editions reaching into the hundreds of thousands of dollars.

- Rare action figures

Certain toys from franchises like Star Wars, Transformers, and He-Man have seen significant appreciation in value, especially those released in the 1970s and 1980s. Vintage action figures in their original packaging are especially sought after. For example, a 1978 Star Wars Boba Fett action figure still in its box can easily sell for over $10,000. The market for these items is highly developed, with rare pieces breaking records at auction year after year.

- Video game memorabilia

The video game memorabilia market is experiencing a significant surge, transitioning from a niche interest to a mainstream investment opportunity. This growth is fueled by the increasing popularity of gaming, the rise of e-commerce, and the growing acceptance of gaming as a legitimate form of entertainment.

Rare and vintage items are at the forefront of this trend. For instance, a sealed copy of *Super Mario Bros.* for the NES sold for a record £1.5 million in 2021, highlighting the immense value collectors place on pristine, early-edition games. Similarly, the gold Nintendo World Championships 1990 cartridge has fetched over £160,000, underscoring the demand for limited-production items tied to significant gaming events.

Consoles also play a pivotal role in this market. Original units like the NES, SNES, and Atari 2600 can command thousands of dollars, especially when in excellent condition or featuring unique color variants. The allure of these items is not just their functionality, but their nostalgic value and cultural significance in the gaming community.

The market's expansion is further supported by platforms like eBay, which saw a 330% increase in sales of graded video games between February 2020 and June 2025. This growth is indicative of a broader trend where collectors and investors are increasingly turning to video game memorabilia as a viable and profitable asset class.

- Pokémon

The Pokémon franchise began as a video game and exploded into a global cultural phenomenon, with one of the largest and most dedicated fan bases in the world. Pokémon memorabilia, including trading cards, plush toys, and video games, has seen massive increases in value over the years.

Pokémon trading cards in particular, have become incredibly valuable, with rare cards like the First Edition

Charizard fetching hundreds of thousands of dollars at auction. Collectors are also increasingly investing in sealed packs of Pokémon cards, with some packs selling for tens of thousands of dollars due to their rarity and nostalgia value. As the Pokémon franchise continues to release new content- whether through video games, trading cards, or other media- demand for Pokémon memorabilia is expected to keep growing.

- Funko pop

Shows like Stranger Things, The Witcher, and other Netflix hits have begun to inspire collectible items, but this area of memorabilia is still developing. Funko Pop figures and limited-edition merchandise from these shows are just getting started. As these franchises grow in popularity, expect memorabilia from these fandoms to rise in value, especially as limited runs of merchandise hit the market. Collectors who spot these trends early may reap huge rewards down the road.

Blockbuster films, comic book universes, and video game franchises are showing no signs of slowing down in growth. Items tied to these properties will likely become even more valuable over time. According to a report by The Hollywood Reporter, the global film industry reached a record $100 billion in revenue in 2023, with Marvel Studios alone contributing $23 billion in box office earnings since its inception in 2008. This success has rippled through the memorabilia market, with items related to these movies increasing in value. The market for these collectibles has surged as both casual and hardcore fans seek to own a piece of these beloved universes.

Plus, the market for streaming show collectibles is emerging, offering new opportunities for collectors to invest in a wide range of memorabilia. According to Statista, in 2023

Netflix alone reached over 230 million subscribers globally, contributing to the massive fandoms around its original shows. While the market for streaming-related memorabilia is still in its early stages, it is growing fast. For instance, the Stranger Things franchise, which has enjoyed massive success and multiple seasons, has spawned Funko Pops, limited-edition board games, and art prints. As these shows gain more cultural relevance, the collectibles tied to them are expected to see an increase in value.

Heritage Auctions, Hake's Auctions, and Goldin Auctions dominate high-value sales for pop culture memorabilia, often specializing in comic books, action figures, and retro games. ComicConnect and Metropolis Collectibles are renowned for their focus on comic books, having brokered record-setting sales like *Action Comics #1* for $3.2 million. eBay remains a massive secondary market for low-to-mid-tier collectibles, though high-end buyers typically prefer authenticated, verified channels.

To authenticate memorabilia within this category, Wata Games- which specializes in grading and sealing retro video games- is a great place for value validation (e.g., *Super Mario Bros.* sold for $2 million with a Wata 9.8 A+ rating). CGC (Certified Guaranty Company) is the gold standard in comic book grading; their 10-point scale directly influences price. Beckett Authentication Services and PSA also certify autographs and collectibles, adding trust and liquidity to the market.

Conventions and fan expos are major engines behind the growth of pop culture memorabilia. These events drive collector engagement, unveil rare pieces, and connect fans to vendors and auction houses. Here are some of the biggest:

1. San Diego Comic-Con International (SDCC)

   Happens every July in San Diego Convention Center, California

   The biggest pop culture event in the world. Premieres exclusive collectibles, variant comic covers, and limited-edition toys. A launchpad for rising values.

2. New York Comic Con (NYCC)

   Takes place every October at the Javits Center, NYC

   Massive showcase of comic memorabilia, celebrity signings, and exclusives from major franchises like Marvel, DC, and Pokémon.

3. Toy Fair New York

   It happens annually in February at the Jacob Javits Center, NYC

   Collectors and retailers preview the year's biggest toy trends. While primarily industry-focused, it sparks demand across the memorabilia ecosystem.

4. Power-Con

   It takes place in August in Columbus, Ohio

   Focused on vintage toy lines like He-Man, GI Joe, and Transformers. A hub for rare vintage toy auctions and collectors.

5. RetroGameCon & Classic Gaming Expo

   It's annual, but the time varies by year. It's staged in U.S. cities like Syracuse, Portland, and Las Vegas

   Great place for video game memorabilia enthusiasts - NES, Sega, Atari, and rare arcade items. Collectors meet Wata-graded games face-to-face.

Table 5: Most Expensive Pop-Culture Memorabilia of All Time

ITEM	TYPE	PRICE	YEAR OF SALE	ADDITIONAL INFO
Action Comics #1 (Superman's First Appearance)	Comic Book	$3.2 million	2014	Widely regarded as the most valuable comic ever sold. Marks Superman's 1938 debut.
Super Mario Bros. NES Sealed Copy	Video Game	$2 million	2021	A sealed, near-mint copy graded 9.8 A+ by Wata Games. Set a new standard in retro game collecting.
The Amazing Spider-Man #1	Comic Book	$1.1 million	2011	The first standalone Spider-Man issue, highlighting the rise of Marvel's most iconic character.
Star Wars Stormtrooper Helmet (Limited Edition)	Merchandise	$500,000	2017	A high-end, limited replica of the iconic helmet from the *Star Wars* franchise. A top-tier collectible in sci-fi memorabilia.

Sources: Heritage Auctions, Wata Games, Julien's Auctions.

The memorabilia space- whether sports, entertainment, historical, political, or pop culture-has evolved into a thriving market, one where unique artifacts from the past command ever-increasing prices. From the sale of an original Super Mario Bros. NES cartridge for a staggering $2 million to a pair of blood-stained gloves worn by Abraham Lincoln fetching $68,000, the market is full of surprises. But what lies beneath these headline-grabbing sales? How have these markets evolved, and what trends are shaping the future of collectible memorabilia?

To understand the market dynamics and trends in this field, one has to examine several key factors including: rarity, cultural significance, emotional value, and the growing influence of new technologies. Collectors, investors, and enthusiasts alike are reshaping what we consider valuable, and the forces at play in this space are transforming the ways in which we engage with and invest in memorabilia. The next chapter will consider these market drivers and explore how they've influenced the trends in both established and emerging collectible categories.

Collectible & Memorabilia Market Dynamics and Trends

KEY INSIGHTS

- The memorabilia market is US-driven and is booming. It is valued at over $6 billion in the US alone and is rapidly expanding worldwide. Demand is soaring across the US, Europe, Asia, and Latin America.

- Limited availability of items combined with powerful emotional connections to the past are primary drivers. Scarcity elevates value.

- Memorabilia linked to culturally significant figures and current trends command premium prices.

- Authentication and grading by trusted third parties are critical for market confidence, helping legitimize memorabilia as a credible investment class.

- Fractionalization is revolutionizing the market by allowing investors to own shares of high-value memorabilia, breaking down barriers of entry and enabling broader participation in assets once limited to the ultra-wealthy.

The memorabilia market is an exciting and rapidly evolving industry, driven by a fascinating mix of cultural, economic, and technological forces. As the demand for collectible items continues to soar, understanding the trends and market dynamics is essential for anyone looking to tap into this lucrative space. From iconic sports memorabilia to rare pop culture artifacts, this market is teeming with opportunities, and the time to invest has never been more promising.

The US has long been the beating heart of the memorabilia market, leading the charge with both financial might and cultural influence. With an annual valuation of over $6 billion, according to the 2025 Sports Collectors Digest report, the US market is an epicenter for everything from autographed jerseys and trading cards to vintage pop culture pieces and historical treasures. But it's not just collectors who are getting in on the action, wealthy investors are increasingly eyeing memorabilia as a profitable asset class.

The numbers speak for themselves. Between 2019 and 2021, the memorabilia sector experienced an eye-popping 25% year-on-year growth, outpacing other alternative investment options (IBISWorld, 2024). This rapid expansion has positioned memorabilia as one of the most exciting and fast-growing investment opportunities today. Whether you're a seasoned investor or someone just beginning to explore alternative assets, the memorabilia market is offering unprecedented potential for those who are ready to dive in.

The Globalization of Memorabilia

The memorabilia market is US-driven, but is rapidly expanding across the globe, offering exciting investment opportunities that span continents and cultures.

Europe is a key player in the memorabilia market, accounting for approximately 25% of the global market share (Verified Market Reports). In this region, sports memorabilia make up about 40% of sales, with items tied to major events like the FIFA World Cup, or to iconic football clubs like

Barcelona and Manchester United. Art-related collectibles, including rare paintings and sculptures, are also hugely popular, making up 30% of the European memorabilia market.

In the UK, football (soccer) memorabilia from legendary players like Pelé has seen prices skyrocket into the millions (Seidman, 2018). A Maradona jersey worn during the 1986 World Cup was sold at Sotheby's for $9.3 million in 2022, setting a new benchmark for football memorabilia. This surge in demand is reflective of the global love for sports icons, with similar spikes in interest across the world.

The international reach of sports, particularly soccer, basketball, and baseball, has propelled the growth of cross-border demand for memorabilia tied to athletes and teams from around the world. This is a golden era for international sports fans, with demand for global superstar memorabilia on the rise.

But it's not just Western collectibles making waves. In China, India, and Southeast Asia, there is an increasing interest in both Western and locally produced memorabilia. In 2025, the Asian memorabilia market is expected to account for a remarkable 20% of global market share, with Japan, China, and South Korea leading the charge in cultural and sports collectibles (Verified Market Reports). This expansion presents a golden opportunity for investors seeking to diversify their portfolios with unique, high-growth assets from emerging markets.

In Japan, the memorabilia market has shifted toward anime and manga, with iconic items from franchises like Dragon Ball Z and One Piece commanding impressive value. A Dragon Ball Z original animation cell *(Plate 3.1)* was sold at Heritage auctions for over $80,000 in 2023 auction. This is part of a broader trend where Eastern collectibles are gaining ground globally, attracting collectors far beyond Asia.

Latin America also boasts a growing memorabilia market, contributing 5% of global sales, with a heavy focus on sports and pop culture items. Collectibles related to soccer legends like Brazil's Pelé and Argentina's Maradona are in high demand, and the region is quickly becoming an essential part of the global memorabilia landscape.

However, for investors, the US remains the central hub for high-profile auctions. Renowned institutions like Sotheby's, Christie's, and Heritage Auctions are regularly setting new records for memorabilia sales, with high-value items fetching millions, like the baseball card of Babe Ruth that sold for a staggering $6 million in 2022, showing how some collectibles are appreciating at rates far beyond traditional assets.

With an increasing number of cross-cultural exchanges, a growing international community of collectors, and skyrocketing demand, the memorabilia market offers a unique opportunity for anyone looking to diversify their investments. This is how the memorabilia market is divided globally. Appendix 2 provides the figures for further review.

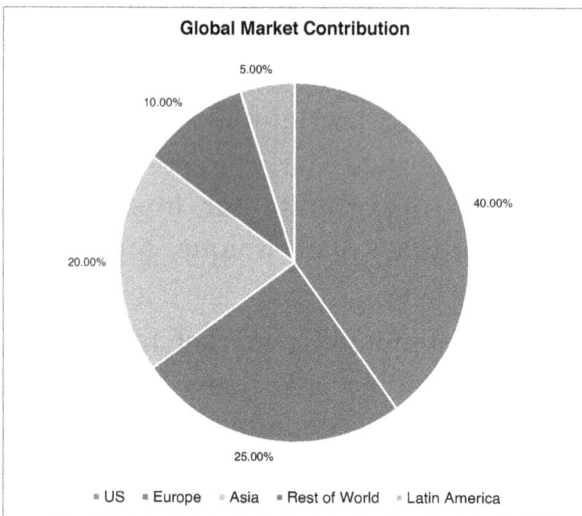

Global Market Contribution

5.00%
10.00%
40.00%
20.00%
25.00%

■ US ■ Europe ■ Asia ■ Rest of World ■ Latin America

Figure 3: Global Memorabilia Market

Source: Verified Market Reports, 2023

Key Drivers of Demand

1. Scarcity

Scarcity has long been one of the most powerful drivers behind the demand for collectible memorabilia. The concept is simple: the fewer there are of an item, the more desirable it becomes. Whether it's due to limited production runs, historical significance, or inherent uniqueness, scarcity elevates the perceived value of items. Collectors and investors are drawn to the idea of owning something rare- an artifact that has personal, historical, or cultural meaning and is hard to come by.

There are countless examples of athletes whose iconic items have achieved astronomical prices because of their scarcity. Babe Ruth's memorabilia hold immense value due to both his historical significance and the scarcity of items associated with him. A jersey he wore during the 1919 season when he played for the Boston Red Sox sold at auction for $4.4 million in 2012. Only a handful of items tied to Ruth from this era exist, and as a result, the prices of those rare pieces are extraordinarily high.

In February 2022, Tom Brady announced his retirement (only to unretire weeks later), and a football he threw during what was believed to be his final touchdown pass sold for $518,000 at auction. However, after Brady returned to the NFL, the ball's value dropped significantly. It was no longer as scarce once he was playing again.

Rare coins, especially those that have been in circulation for hundreds of years or are one of a kind, are another example of how scarcity drives value. One of the most famous examples of a rare coin is the 1933 $20 Double Eagle coin. Although the U.S. government minted over 445,000 of these coins, they were never released into circulation, and nearly all were destroyed. A small number of the coins managed to survive, and in 2002, one was sold for a staggering $7.6 million at Stack's Bowers Galleries in New York. Its scarcity-fewer than a dozen coins are believed to exist-combined with its historical significance, makes it one of the most expensive coins ever sold.

The story of the 1794 Flowing Hair Dollar is similar. It is widely regarded as one of the first silver dollars minted by the U.S. government. Only a handful of these coins remain, and in 2013, one was sold at Stack's Bowers Galleries for $10 million, making it the most expensive coin ever sold. The combination of rarity, historical importance, and the sheer uniqueness of having one of the first U.S. government-issued coins drove its price to unprecedented levels.

2. Nostalgia

People have an innate desire to reconnect with moments from their past, to relive the emotions tied to formative experiences, and to keep memories alive through tangible items. As society evolves and time passes, this connection to the past only intensifies, leading to a booming market for items that evoke memories of childhood, youth, or significant cultural milestones. For many, memorabilia is not merely an object; it is a vessel for emotional experiences and a way to temporarily re-live a time when life felt simpler or more carefree.

Nostalgia-driven purchases are particularly prevalent in sectors like music memorabilia, pop culture, automotive collectibles, and toys from past generations. Items that remind consumers of past eras, whether they grew up in the '60s, '70s, '80s, or the more recent '90s and early 2000s, often carry an emotional weight that transcends their material value. As people become more affluent and settled in their lives, the desire to reconnect with the things that shaped their identity intensifies.

Vinyl records have seen a resurgence in recent years, thanks in part to their nostalgic appeal. For Baby Boomers and Generation X, vinyl represents a time when music was experienced in a more physical, ritualistic way. Listening to a record on a turntable was not just about the music; it was an immersive experience. Many people are now rediscovering that tactile pleasure, with vintage vinyl records from artists like The Beatles, Pink Floyd, or Led Zeppelin in high demand.

In 2021, a rare copy of The Beatles' White Album signed by all four members sold for $790,000 at Julien's auctions. This iconic piece of musical history is a perfect example of how memorabilia from the past can hold immense value not just because of its rarity, but because it evokes powerful memories tied to a transformative cultural moment. While for Millennials and Gen Z this resurgence of interest in vinyl may be less about personal nostalgia and more about the experience of vintage audio, it is still rooted in the cultural reverence of past music eras.

Posters from the '60s and '70s, particularly from iconic venues like the Fillmore in San Francisco or the Whisky a Go Go in Los Angeles, can fetch tens of thousands of dollars today because of nostalgia. The imagery of these vintage posters' transports people to the heyday of rock and roll, when bands like The Doors, Jimi Hendrix, and The Grateful Dead ruled the stage.

Similarly, tickets from major events such as the Woodstock Festival or the original Live Aid concert hold a special kind of nostalgia. These items are more than just mementos; they are windows into cultural milestones that many consumers want to relive.

For many car enthusiasts, vintage vehicles are more than just transportation, they represent a golden age of design, innovation, and craftsmanship. Cars from the mid-20th century such as the 1960s Ford Mustang, the 1957 Chevrolet Corvette, or the 1969 Porsche 911, are prime examples of nostalgia-driven collectibles. These cars often serve as a link to the past, reminding owners of the era when these vehicles were at the height of their popularity.

3. Cultural relevance

Items that are tied to current events or highly relevant cultural phenomena often gain value due to their resonance with contemporary audiences. For example, the sports jerseys of rising stars like LeBron James or Serena Williams can quickly appreciate in value due to their real-time cultural impact. Similarly, collectibles linked to pop culture moments such as movies, TV shows, or video games are more likely to gain interest when those cultural forces are in the limelight.

It will matter who the attached athlete is for sport memorabilia, for example. Was the athlete or the era they played in historically impactful? Did they revolutionize their sport, set records, or influence pop culture beyond the game? Michael Jordan's legendary status, for example, makes any memorabilia tied to him highly sought after. His 1984 Air Ships, which he wore in his early rookie games, sold for an incredible $1.472 million at a Sotheby's in 2021. That kind of demand doesn't just come from the sneakers themselves but from Jordan's larger-than-life impact on basketball and pop culture.

The increasing importance of popular franchises such as Marvel, Star Wars, or Harry Potter has propelled memorabilia from these domains into high demand, further fueling market growth.

Notably, the growing influence of celebrity culture has also had a significant impact on memorabilia markets. Autographed items, personal items, or objects connected to major celebrities are increasingly valuable. High-profile figures like Beyoncé, Taylor Swift, and Leonardo DiCaprio have raised the profile of their memorabilia, leading to increasing auction prices.

There has also been a rise of digital and online celebrities such as YouTubers, streamers and influencers, and so there is a growing market for memorabilia associated with these people. Items such as merchandise, limited-edition content, and digital assets related to influencers have started to attract considerable attention from younger generations. This shift is changing the traditional celebrity-driven dynamics of memorabilia markets and is an area that is likely to grow as influencer culture continues to thrive.

4. Credibility

As the value of memorabilia skyrockets and more investors pour into the space, the need for trust, transparency, and expert authentication has never been greater. And that's exactly where third-party independent graders and valuators come in. These organizations have revolutionized the way collectors and investors approach high-value items.

Companies like PSA, Beckett Grading Services (BGS), SGC, and JSA (James Spence Authentication) have become household names among serious collectors. Their role is simple, but essential: verify authenticity, assign objective condition grades, and provide consistent, reliable documentation that gives buyers confidence. When an item is graded and encapsulated by a respected third party, it instantly gains legitimacy-and in most cases, value.

This isn't just about slabbing a card. It's about removing doubt, which in turn is a massive driver of demand and price appreciation. Whether it's a game-used jersey or an autographed baseball, collectors want assurance that what they're buying is 100% the real deal. A PSA 10? That's a gold standard. A jersey authenticated by MeiGray or Fanatics Authentic? That's the type of proof that investors are looking for.

The rise of these grading and authentication services has also made the market more accessible to newcomers. Buyers who may not have decades of experience can rely on professional grading to guide their purchases. It levels the playing field and brings credibility to every transaction, whether you're dropping $100 or $1 million.

Even in emerging markets like NFTs and digital collectibles, the concept of independent validation is being carried over, only now it's via blockchain verification and smart contracts. That just goes to show how deep this need for trust runs across the entire memorabilia ecosystem. Institutions that help validate and protect memorabilia investment have made the market stronger, more mature, and ready for long-term growth.

5. Rise as an investment class

In recent years, memorabilia has increasingly been viewed not just as a collector's item, but as a viable investment asset. Like fine art, rare wine, or classic cars, memorabilia has proven its potential to appreciate significantly over time. High-profile auction sales, where items routinely exceed their expected values, have contributed to this shift in perception. Collectors and investors alike are now treating these items as portfolio diversifiers, seeking opportunities to acquire pieces that will appreciate over the long term.

Items tied to historically significant events and figures, like autographed sports memorabilia or rare music items, are seeing strong investment demand. For instance, rare jerseys worn by athletes such as Michael Jordan or Kobe Bryant, or signed albums by artists like The Beatles, are attracting investors looking for tangible assets that offer both cultural and financial value. Additionally, the rise of fractional ownership, where collectors can own shares in high-value items, is making it easier for investors to access these markets without requiring the capital to buy entire pieces.

6. Mainstream players entering the market

As demand for memorabilia continues to grow, mainstream players from outside the traditional collectibles' world are entering the space and recognizing the potential for profit. Companies like Fanatics, with its strong foothold in sports merchandising, have extended into the memorabilia sector, investing heavily in authentication and grading services. The entry of these major companies signals a shift toward professionalization in the industry, making the market more organized and accessible to collectors and investors alike.

This influx of mainstream players also drives the expansion of the market itself. As bigger corporations enter the field, they not only inject financial capital, but also bring a level of legitimacy to the industry, attracting a more diverse and affluent consumer base. The ability to scale operations, utilize digital platforms, and create new revenue streams has allowed companies to profit from the growing demand for memorabilia, ensuring the market's continued growth. This trend of corporate involvement is expected to further fuel the increasing mainstream appeal of memorabilia as both a collectible and an investment.

7. Social media's influence

Social media has become a critical driver of demand in the memorabilia space. Platforms like Instagram, TikTok, X, and Facebook have amplified the visibility of rare items, fueling desire and creating bidding wars. Collectors, celebrities, and influencers are all leveraging these platforms to share their collections, creating a ripple effect across their followers and encouraging fans to seek out similar pieces.

The viral nature of social media means that items can quickly go from being relatively unknown to highly coveted. For instance, when a celebrity or high-profile figure shares a rare piece of memorabilia, it can skyrocket in value overnight, particularly if it's tied to a moment in pop culture. Hashtags like #memorabilia, #collectibles, and #sportscollecting have created niche communities that continually discuss, promote, and elevate certain collectibles, making them even more desirable. This grassroots exposure, coupled with the constant stream of content, is playing a major role in driving demand.

Furthermore, social media has democratized the memorabilia market, allowing enthusiasts from all over the world to connect, share, and trade items. Live auctions and sales events are now frequently streamed, with real-time engagement driving competition and pushing prices higher, as audiences feel more connected to the process.

8. Technology

The impact of technology on the memorabilia market cannot be understated. From online marketplaces to blockchain-based authentication systems, technology is expanding the reach of the market and enabling new forms of ownership and transaction. Digital platforms such as eBay, Goldin Auctions, and Sotheby's have allowed collectors to buy and sell memorabilia from anywhere in the world, vastly increasing the market's reach and accessibility.

The integration of blockchain technology is also helping to ensure the authenticity and provenance of items, addressing one of the biggest concerns in the memorabilia market. By creating verifiable and tamper-proof records, blockchain is reassuring collectors and investors about the legitimacy of their purchases. This new form of digital ownership- especially of rare or high-value items- has opened up a wealth of possibilities for memorabilia collectors, allowing them to securely and transparently trade items across borders.

Virtual reality (VR) and augmented reality (AR) are also beginning to make their mark on the industry. Companies are exploring ways to offer virtual experiences where collectors can view and interact with high-end memorabilia digitally. For instance, potential buyers can virtually "try on" a famous actor's costumes or inspect a historic item from multiple angles before making a purchase. These technologies are enhancing the collector's experience and making it easier for buyers and sellers to interact in entirely new ways, expanding the possibilities for memorabilia trading in the future.

The Rise of Fractionalization

In recent years, fractionalization has become popular as a groundbreaking solution to the challenge of affording expensive memorabilia, making high-value assets more accessible to a broader range of investors and enthusiasts. This concept allows multiple people to own a fraction of a prized piece of memorabilia by dividing ownership into shares. As a result, it democratizes the ownership of previously unattainable artifacts, allowing fans, collectors, and investors to participate in markets that were once exclusive to the ultra-wealthy.

This movement can be traced to several factors: soaring prices in collectible markets, the increasing appeal of collectibles as an alternative investment vehicle, and to some degree the advent of blockchain technology. Items like autographed sports jerseys, vintage baseball cards, or iconic sneakers have seen market prices skyrocket in recent years, pricing out all but the wealthiest collectors. By fractionalizing these assets, platforms enable investors to purchase small portions of an item, thereby spreading the cost across multiple stakeholders. Each shareholder can participate in the potential future appreciation of the item, without needing to pay the full market price upfront.

Several key players have risen to prominence in this market, helping to shape its rapid growth and popularity. Companies such as Rally and Otis have led the way by allowing users to buy shares in everything from signed sports memorabilia to rare watches and fine art. These platforms typically acquire valuable collectibles, authenticate them, and then issue shares to the public, giving investors a stake in the asset's future value. Through these companies, fractional ownership is accessible through user-friendly interfaces, making it easy for newcomers to join the market.

Rally, for instance, has attracted significant attention by offering shares in items like a 1952 Mickey Mantle rookie card, or an original comic book featuring Spider-Man's debut. Similarly, Otis has made waves by allowing investors to buy shares in high-end sneakers, luxury handbags, and even a segment of musical history, such as Elvis Presley's leather jacket. Both platforms offer a blend of investment and memorabilia collecting, where investors not only have financial incentives but also a connection to their favorite pieces of history.

Fractionalization has transformed the way investors and collectors view high-value memorabilia, making it accessible to a wider range of people while offering opportunities for diversification in portfolios. As the market matures and more platforms emerge, it's likely that fractionalization will continue to shape the future of the collectibles space, enabling a new generation of owners to experience the thrill of investing in rare and iconic artifacts.

However, this newfound access doesn't come without trade-offs. Investors, while gaining financial exposure, must often surrender the emotional experience of tangible ownership - there's no framed jersey on the wall or signed glove in a case. The asset lives in a vault, secured and insured, but physically distant. In this way, fractionalization alters not just how we invest in a piece, but how we relate to it.

And the risks extend beyond sentiment. With low barriers to entry and limited regulation, fractional platforms are still finding their footing. If one collapses, the fate of the stored collectibles and their investors can become tangled in legal and logistical uncertainty. The market itself is also young; secondary trading is possible but not always liquid, and valuations can be volatile, driven more by fandom than fundamentals.

Yet the innovation unfolding here is undeniable. Blockchain technology is beginning to offer more secure, transparent proof of ownership, and hybrid models are emerging where digital tokens are tied to physical assets. Imagine owning a share of Muhammad Ali's training robe, with both physical custody in a museum and a blockchain certificate in your wallet. It's this kind of fusion that may anchor trust and scalability.

Looking forward, institutions could reshape the model entirely. Museums may one day offer public ownership of artifacts in exchange for preservation funding, and cultural institutions across the world could turn passive spectators into active stakeholders. As platforms expand globally and AI-powered valuation tools refine pricing models, fractionalization may become a standard rather than a novelty - just another way for individuals to own, invest in, and preserve the icons that define our history.

In the end, this isn't just about finance. It's about access, identity, and connection. Fractional ownership offers something new: the ability to be part of something legendary; not by proximity or privilege, but by choice.

Investment and Speculation in Memorabilia

Since collectibles are becoming a legitimate investment asset class, many high-net-worth people and institutions are starting to see rare memorabilia as a store of value, much like fine art, vintage cars, or real estate. It has been evident in the way items such as trading cards, sports jerseys, and comic books have appreciated in value by several hundred percent in recent years.

Sports cards, specifically, have experienced an investment boom. According to The Wall Street Journal, the market for sports cards alone was valued at $5.4 billion in 2021 and is projected to grow substantially. There are now dedicated investment funds that focus on the memorabilia sector, and many collectors are diversifying their portfolios by investing in high-value collectibles.

Fractionalization is attracting a new breed of collectors who may not have the financial means to purchase entire assets, but want to participate in the potential upside of memorabilia investment. The next section of this book will help you understand how you, too, can be part of this revolution.

Plate 1.1 - 1952 Topps Mickey Mantle **Source:** *Heritage Auctions*	Plate 1.2 - Babe Ruth's 1932 Jersey **Source:** *Heritage Auctions*	Plate 1.3 - 1962 Ferrari 250 GTO **Source:** *RM Sotheby's*	Plate 1.4 - 1933 Double Eagle gold coin **Source:** *Square Moose*
Plate 1.5 – Leonardo's Salvator Mundi **Source:** *Time.com*	Plate 1.6 – 1926 Fine & Rare Macallan **Source:** *The Macallan*	Plate 1.7 - Flint hand axe **Source:** *JPost*	Plate 1.8 - T. Rex Stan **Source:** *NY Times*
Plate 1.9 - Guennol Lioness **Source:** *Ancient Pages*	Plate 1.10 - Egyptian Necklace **Source:** *National Jeweler*	Plate 1.11 - Shroud of Turin **Source:** *Wikipedia*	Plate 1.12 – Star Wars Lightsaber **Source:** *Reuters*

Plate 1.13 - Penny Black Stamp **Source:** *Wikipedia*	Plate 2.1 - Michael Jordan's 'Last Dance' Jersey **Source:** *CNBC*	Plate 2.2 - Signed Rusell Wilson Helmet **Source:** *Fanatics Authentic*	Plate 2.3 - Diego Maradona's Hand of God Jersey **Source:** *ESPN*
Plate 2.4 - Erling Haaland UEFA Card *Source: Wikipedia*	Plate 2.5 - Lewis Hamilton Card **Source:** *Wikipedia*	Plate 2.6 - Dorothy Ruby's Slippers **Source:** *Heritage Auctions*	Plate 2.7 - 1966 Batmobile **Source:** *The Guardian*
Plate 2.8 - George Washington's signed letter **Source:** *Raab Collection*	Plate 2.9 - First-edition Pokémon Charizard **Source:** *CNN*	Plate 3.1 - Dragon Ball Animation Plate **Source:** *Heritage Auctions*	Plate 3.2 - 1794 Flowing hair dollar **Source:** *Coin week*

Part II:
INVESTING IN
MEMORABILIA

Early in 2025, an iconic sports figure stepped into the world of sports memorabilia not just as a collector, but as an investor and a curator of history. Tom Brady made headlines by purchasing a 50% stake in a Boston-based sports card and memorabilia chain, which has since been rebranded as CardVault by Brady. This move didn't just signify an interest in collectible items, it was Brady's way of intertwining his lifelong passion for sports memorabilia with his entrepreneurial spirit, setting the stage for fans to engage with the history of sports differently than before.

The Retailer, which was founded in 2020, had already carved out a unique niche for itself, with locations inside iconic venues like TD Garden, Gillette Stadium, and Foxwoods Resort Casino. As of the time of the purchase, the store was slated to open another venue near MetLife Stadium in New Jersey. The company has ambitions to go even further, with plans to expand across the U.S. and even into international markets, thanks to Brady's involvement.

Why would one of the greatest quarterbacks in history choose to invest in sports cards and memorabilia? When asked, Brady said that collectibles and cards had been part of his DNA since childhood. For him, this was not just about buying and selling cards, but curating history, building community, and allowing fans to own a piece of iconic moments in sports.

There is an increasing recognition of the value of memorabilia, not just as a hobby, but as a legitimate investment. This section of the book will make it all real for you. It will help you see why you should invest in memorabilia and how to go about it.

This book often talks about collectors and investors, and while the two are different, they do overlap. A collector buys with their heart; they chase what they love, it's about passion, emotion, and a connection to history. An investor, on the other hand, is thinking about ROI; what will appreciate, when to buy, when to sell, and how to manage risk. In today's market however, you can be both. The smartest people in the space are building collections they love that also increase in value. This section will help you develop an investor mindset wrapped inside a collector's heart.

You'll learn about short-term and long-term investing. Short-term investing is all about hype, timing, and momentum, a breakout rookie season, a viral moment, or a retirement announcement. Think of when Tom Brady retired in 2022 (the *first* time), prices of his cards and memorabilia spiked instantly. Some smart investors sold into that moment; that's a short-term play. Long-term investing, on the other hand, involves blue-chip collectibles. Items with enduring value, historical significance, and cultural weight. It involves pieces that appreciate steadily over time, regardless of market fads.

You want to ride the wave of hype sometimes, but also build a collection that holds weight 10, 20, 30 years from now, to invest in both legacy and popularity.

Why Invest in Memorabilia?

KEY INSIGHTS

- Memorabilia beats traditional assets, offering strong returns, especially during downturns. Its value isn't tied to stocks, reducing overall portfolio risk.

- Patience turns rare items into multi-million-dollar treasures. Collect what you love and profit while enjoying it.

- Know the risks - Fraud, storage, and hype can hurt your portfolio, but smart strategies protect you. Research, authenticate, and hold steady to build legacy. Over the past decade, something remarkable has been happening in the world of investing, quietly, steadily, and without the bells and whistles that often accompany tech IPOs or Wall Street rallies. While headlines focused on stock surges and crypto crashes, a quieter asset class has been delivering returns that are not just competitive, but in many cases, superior to traditional investments.

Long seen as the domain of passionate collectors and die-hard fans, the memorabilia market has snuck through the back door and begun to assert itself as a legitimate financial asset class. From the nostalgia-fueled boom of the pandemic years to today's steady growth across high-end collectibles, memorabilia has demonstrated an uncanny ability to preserve value, and even thrive, during periods of economic uncertainty.

Let's look at the numbers.

The figure below (Figure 4) compares estimated average annual returns across several major asset classes. The performance of sports memorabilia and luxury watches stands out in particular, challenging the dominance of more traditional investments like stocks, real estate, and bonds.

Keep in mind that these figures are estimates based on aggregate historical data and should be interpreted as indicative, not exact.

- Sports memorabilia data is less standardized and more volatile, so estimates are based on auction results and index proxies like the PWCC 500.
- Luxury watches are primarily based on secondary market prices (e.g. Rolex, Patek Philippe (*Plate 4.1*)) from platforms like Chrono24 and WatchCharts.
- S&P 500, REITs, and Treasury Bonds are based on historical index data (e.g. SPY, VNQ, and average bond yields).
- For those interested in exploring the underlying figures, the raw data is available in Appendix 2.

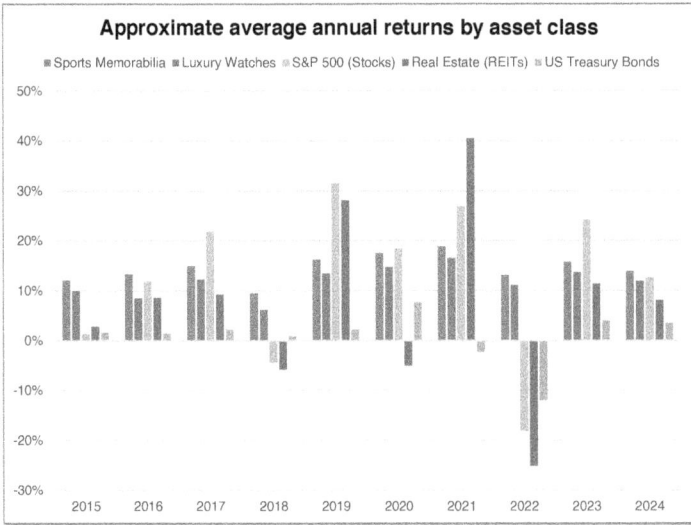

Approximate average annual returns by asset class

■ Sports Memorabilia ■ Luxury Watches ■ S&P 500 (Stocks) ■ Real Estate (REITs) ■ US Treasury Bonds

Figure 4: Approximate Average Annual Returns by Asset Class Over the Last Decade

Source: Compiled using data from PWCC Market Index, Chrono24, Watch Charts, Yahoo Finance, and U.S. Treasury yield archives.

One of the most compelling attributes of memorabilia is its resilience during economic downturns. When traditional markets tumbled in 2008, high-grade memorabilia didn't just hold its ground, it gained ground. The iconic T206 Honus Wagner card *(Plate 4.2)* for example, appreciated significantly during that decade. A PSA 2-graded Wagner sold for $75,000 in 2000, by 2008 its value had skyrocketed to $791,000.

This trend repeated itself during the COVID-19 pandemic. While global markets endured sharp volatility, the memorabilia market experienced a renaissance. The PWCC Top 100 Index, which tracks elite-grade trading cards, rose an astounding 264% between 2008 and 2020. And the momentum didn't stop there.

In 2020, a 1952 Topps Mickey Mantle card fetched $5.2 million. By 2022, another version of that same card sold for a staggering $12.6 million, setting a new benchmark for the entire category. These aren't just isolated events, they're reflective of a larger trend: the growing recognition of memorabilia as a store of value and a vehicle for wealth generation.

To really understand how sports memorabilia stack up, take a look at its performance versus the S&P 500 between 2000 and 2024.

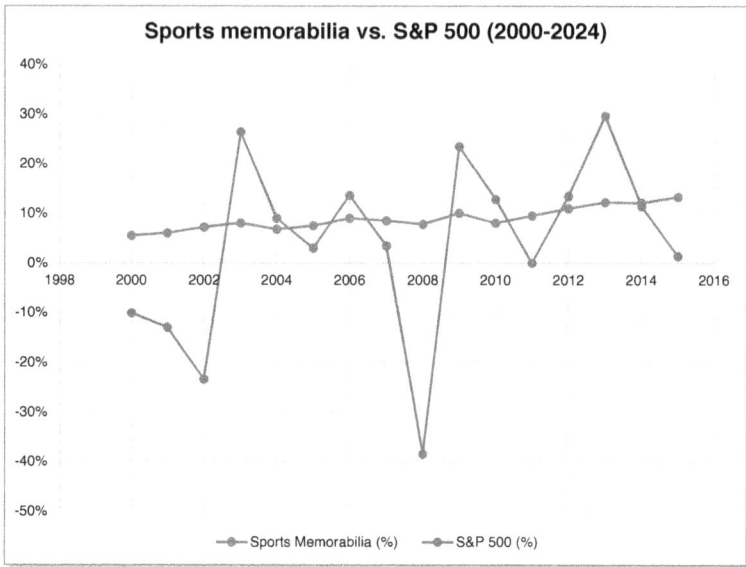

Figure 5: Comparative Annual Returns for Sports Memorabilia Vs. S&P 500 (2000-2024)
Source: Compiled using data from PWCC Market Index, Heritage Auctions, SPY performance via Yahoo Finance, and analyst estimates. See Appendix 2 for the full dataset (2000–2024).

While stocks have traditionally been viewed as the default growth vehicle, sports memorabilia have consistently delivered impressive returns, -notably with much less downside during crises. This positions memorabilia not only as a growth asset but as a hedge against economic volatility.

Based on this data, these are the key reasons to invest in memorabilia:

- Memorabilia often retains or increases in value during economic downturns, offering a hedge against market volatility.

- Record-breaking sales such as the $12.6 million Mickey Mantle card, highlight the market's potential.

- The global sports memorabilia market alone is projected to reach $271.2 billion by 2034, growing at a CAGR of 22.1%. The whole market at large is growing.

- Including sports memorabilia in an investment portfolio can provide diversification benefits due to its low correlation with traditional assets.

Diversification and Long-Term Returns

When it comes to building a robust investment portfolio, one of the golden rules is diversification. The idea is simple- don't put all your eggs in one basket. When you spread your investments across different asset classes- stocks, bonds, real estate, commodities, and yes, memorabilia- you minimize risks and increase the potential for long-term returns. Memorabilia in particular offer an exciting and unique way to diversify your portfolio, while also tapping into the potential for significant growth.

Most traditional investments, such as stocks or bonds, can be subject to market volatility. Global economic shifts, political instability, and even changes in consumer behavior can cause fluctuations in these markets. But memorabilia is different. While it can still experience its ups and downs, the value of collectibles is often driven by factors unrelated to broader economic trends. This makes it an excellent tool for diversification, because its performance often doesn't correlate directly with the stock market.

Sports memorabilia can rise in value during periods when the stock market is struggling. This is because the demand for rare items like vintage sports cards or signed jerseys is largely influenced by nostalgia, fan loyalty, and the popularity of the athletes or teams associated with those pieces. As more collectors seek to own a piece of history, the market for memorabilia can become somewhat insulated from the swings of the stock market or economic downturns.

Memorabilia also tends to perform better in the long run. While stocks may go up and down day-to-day or even year-to-year, rare collectibles typically appreciate in value over decades. The longer you hold onto certain pieces- especially ones with significant historical relevance or those tied to legendary figures- the more likely they are to increase in worth. This makes memorabilia a smart long-term investment, offering the potential for substantial returns without the worry of daily market fluctuations.

In fact, if you're investing for the long haul, memorabilia can be a great way to build wealth over time. Unlike other assets that might require constant monitoring or active management, memorabilia keeps its appeal, provided it's kept in good condition. Take for example sports trading cards. In the 1980s and early '90s, the market for cards was booming, but many of these cards were produced in high quantities, which led to overproduction and a decline in value. However, as time passed, certain cards from that era- especially those tied to iconic athletes like Michael Jordan, Larry Bird and Tim Duncan - have seen their values skyrocket. Someone who held onto a card from that period did not need to keep monitoring their asset; they simply waited. The owner of the T206 Honus Wagner baseball card (one of the most famous trading cards in the world, which sold for over $6 million in a private sale in 2021 and $7.25 million in 2022), did nothing but wait, and their patience turned their collectible into a multi-million-dollar asset. An interesting aside on this is that as of 2024, there were no publicly reported sales of the T206

Honus Wagner card, marking the first year in three decades without a recorded transaction. This lack of sales is attributed to the card's extreme scarcity and the reluctance of current owners to part with such a valuable asset. No known sale has ever resulted in a loss for the seller.

By including memorabilia in your portfolio, you're reducing your overall risk. If the stock market crashes or your other investments take a hit, your memorabilia might be less affected and could even gain value as other financial assets decline. Over time, many collectibles and rare memorabilia have proven to be excellent long-term investments. Holding on to rare, historical items allows you to capitalize on their growing value as the demand for these pieces increases. Diversifying into memorabilia is a way to protect yourself and position yourself to profit from the rising value of rare and limited-edition items.

Unlike cash, memorabilia has the power to appreciate over time, particularly as interest in certain collectibles increases and rare items become scarcer. Whether it's vintage sports cards, jerseys worn by legends, or iconic memorabilia from historic events, these tangible assets can become significantly more valuable as years go by, especially when stored and maintained well.

Personal Enjoyment

When we think of investing, the first things that come to mind are financial gains, market trends, and long-term returns. But one of the often overlooked and yet incredibly rewarding reasons to invest in memorabilia is the personal enjoyment it brings. There's a unique kind of satisfaction that comes with collecting items that you're passionate about.

Imagine having a collection of rare memorabilia that connects you to a beloved part of your past. Whether it's a vintage comic book, a signed baseball from a legendary player, or a limited-edition poster from your favorite movie, these items are more than just assets, they are tangible links to moments that bring joy, nostalgia, and a sense of connection to something meaningful.

For many investors, the personal enjoyment they derive from their collectibles is just as important as any potential financial returns. If you're someone who loves sports, for instance, owning a jersey worn by your favorite athlete can be an incredibly fulfilling experience. It's not just about the monetary value, -it's about owning a piece of sports history, feeling connected to the athlete and the team, and having a tangible reminder of that passion every day. Every time you look at that jersey, you're not just seeing an asset, you're revisiting memories and emotions tied to a time or event you hold dear.

Similarly, if you're a fan of history or art, owning a rare piece of historical memorabilia or an original artwork can bring immense personal satisfaction. These items often carry with them a sense of connection to a significant moment in time or a beloved cultural figure. And while you're watching your investment grow, you're also enjoying the pleasure of owning something that brings you happiness.

The given here is that you're investing in memorabilia you care about, so it becomes more than just a financial transaction. It becomes about curating a collection that speaks to your interests and passions. Even as the value of your memorabilia increases over time, the enjoyment doesn't fade, and you still have the ability to enjoy your collection in a very personal way. And if you ever decide to part with an item, you can be assured that it will find a home with another passionate collector, ensuring that its legacy continues.

Tax Benefits

The financial upside is that some memorabilia may have tax benefits. This can vary quite a bit depending on the country in which you live and the type of memorabilia you're investing in, but in some cases, certain collectibles can come with tax advantages that make them even more appealing.

In many countries, collectibles are classified as capital assets. This means that when you sell an item for a profit, you may be subject to capital gains tax, just as you would be with other investments like stocks or real estate. However, the tax treatment of collectibles can sometimes be more favorable than other asset classes, depending on the specifics of the investment.

For example, in some jurisdictions in the US, long-term capital gains on collectibles may be taxed at a lower rate than short-term capital gains. In others, tax laws may allow you to offset profits from collectibles against losses in other areas of your portfolio. Plus, because memorabilia is tangible, you have greater control over how it is stored, cared for, and in some cases, sold, in ways that might minimize your tax liability.

Another interesting tax-related perk has to do with donations. In many countries, donating valuable items of memorabilia to museums, educational institutions, or charitable organizations can result in tax deductions. If you happen to be an investor who's also passionate about giving back to a cause, donating a significant item from your collection can reduce your taxable income, which could be a win-win for both you and the recipient organization.

However, it's important to note that tax laws vary widely, and tax benefits related to collectibles are often complex. Depending on where you live, how long you've owned the item, and what kind of collectible it is, your tax situation might differ. Some jurisdictions like the Middle East are tax exempt. That's why it's always a good idea to consult with a tax professional who understands the ins and outs of collectible investments. They can guide you in the best way to structure your purchases, sales, and donations to ensure you're getting the maximum tax benefit.

The Risks of Investing in Memorabilia

While memorabilia is an excellent investment option, as with most investments, sometimes people get burned. That's why if you're going to invest, you need to know the risks and how to protect yourself.

1. Fraud

This is the big one, and it's where many first-timers get taken for a ride. Fake autographs. Counterfeit cards. Game-used items that were never within a mile of a stadium. You name it, someone's tried to fake it. The memorabilia market has matured a lot over the past 20 years, but fraud still exists. And when six and seven-figure sums are on the line, the stakes are too high to rely on trust alone.

That's why authentication matters; every high-end item you deal with needs to be authenticated by industry leaders. Provenance (the documented history of the item) is everything. If the paperwork doesn't check out or the signature doesn't match known exemplars, walk away. In fact, if a deal seems too good to be true, it probably is. And if you're buying from someone without a track record, you're gambling, not investing (more on Fraud in the next chapter).

2. Storage

When you invest in memorabilia, you're not just acquiring history, you're responsible for protecting it.

A rare card can lose half its value if it's got a corner ding. A jersey that fades under sunlight or suffers mold damage in a humid basement is money down the drain.

High-end memorabilia require professional storage. We're talking climate-controlled vaults, museum-grade frames, and proper UV protection. Insurance is a must, especially once your collection hits six figures or more. If you're serious about investing in this space, you need to treat it like a gallery. Because one mistake in storage can turn a gem into junk.

3. Valuation

Unlike stocks, memorabilia doesn't have quarterly earnings or a balance sheet. Valuation is subjective, and while comps (comparable sales) are helpful, no two items are exactly alike.

Take two signed baseballs from Babe Ruth. One has crisp ink and full authentication; the other is slightly smudged and comes with questionable provenance. The price difference could be hundreds of thousands.

That's why expert appraisal is crucial. You can't rely on gut feeling or eBay pricing. You need professionals who know the market, track demand, and understand the subtleties that can add or subtract huge value. Auctions help to reveal pricing and provide a standard.

And keep this in mind; the market moves. What's hot today might cool tomorrow. Trends evolve. New stars rise, and older ones fade from the spotlight. You have to stay informed.

4. Market volatility & speculative bubbles

Memorabilia are not immune to hype cycles.

Just like tech stocks or real estate, the collectibles market can heat up fast and cool down even faster. Think of the pandemic-era boom in trading cards. Prices soared and people made fortunes, but when the rush faded, many latecomers were left holding the bag.

Don't mistake passion for price stability. A spike in demand can inflate values, but sustaining that growth takes long-term collector interest, historical relevance, and cultural staying power. I always tell investors: buy what you believe in. If you wouldn't want to own the item if its value dropped 20%, it's probably not the right investment for you.

Investing in memorabilia can be thrilling, profitable, and deeply rewarding; but it's not for the naïve. It's not about flipping cards or chasing hype, it's about playing the long game with knowledge, patience, and discipline. You need to authenticate, store properly, understand valuation, and be mindful of hype cycles. That's the foundation of a smart memorabilia investor.

People turn $10,000 investments into six-figure paydays. People also lose it all by cutting corners. The difference between the two is due diligence- it is your defense and your offense.

Yes, memorabilia investing comes with its own set of challenges. But every single risk we've covered can be mitigated with knowledge, preparation, and discipline.

- Valuation? Do your research. Use data, not instinct.
- Fraud? Stick with verified sellers and third-party authentication.
- Market volatility? Think long-term and stay diversified.
- Storage? Protect your investment like the asset it is.

This isn't about gambling, it's about strategy. If you do your homework, stay patient, and build your collection with intent, you're not just buying objects, you're acquiring legacy. And in the right hands, legacy pays.

Identifying Value in Memorabilia - The Foundations

KEY INSIGHTS

- Authenticity first - If it's not real, it's worthless. Always verify through trusted third parties.

- Grading is a value multiplier – A PSA 10 can be worth 10x a PSA 8. Grade it, don't guess.

- Rarity drives demand - True, artificial, or contextual scarcity all boost value, but condition matters. Even rare items lose value if damaged.

- Demand is emotional- Media, culture, and timing, shift value. Stay alert and informed to combine authenticity, provenance, rarity, condition, and demand.

- Know your strategy- Flip hype-driven items fast; hold legendary pieces long-term, and make sure to protect your investment. Insure valuable items. Use proper storage and keep documentation.

There's an old saying in the memorabilia business that your memorabilia are only worth the amount someone is willing to pay for it. It's not just a saying; it's the gospel truth. I've seen it all. A signed jersey sitting in someone's closet for years, thought to be just a cool piece of history until the right buyer comes along and suddenly, it's a six-figure auction headline. I've seen a beat-up ticket stub from a legendary game go for more than a luxury vacation, simply because it tells a story. The value isn't just in the item, it's in the emotion, the rarity, the authenticity, the timing, and yes, the demand.

People often ask; "how do you know what something's worth?" The answer is always the same: the market speaks. And if you know how to listen- really listen- you can start to understand what gives a piece of memorabilia its value. In this chapter, you'll learn how to look beyond the object and see what collectors and investors see: the story, the scarcity, the sentiment, and ultimately, the dollars.

Authenticity and Provenance

With memorabilia, authenticity isn't just important, it's everything. It doesn't matter how rare your item is, how beautiful it looks, or how great the story sounds. If you can't prove it's real, it's just a nice-looking fake. Period.

Sometimes collectors burn thousands of dollars chasing deals that were too good to be true, and in almost every case, the item couldn't be authenticated. You wouldn't buy a Picasso without knowing it was painted by Picasso, right? The same logic applies here. Whether it's a Babe Ruth ball, a Jordan rookie, or a Tupac-signed poster, provenance and authentication are non-negotiable.

Provenance is the documented history of an item-where it came from, who owned it, and how it changed hands. It's the story behind the piece, but more importantly, it's the paper trail. The more airtight and traceable that history is, the more confident a buyer can be.

You might hear about a jersey "sourced directly from the team" or a signed photo "from the estate of the artist." That's provenance. It's not enough to say, "my uncle got this at a game in '84", you need documentation: original letters of authenticity (LOAs), photos of the moment it was signed, ticket stubs, team records, even video proof. Every bit of credible detail adds weight to your item's legitimacy and ultimately its value.

Authentication, on the other hand, is the process of verifying that an item is what the seller claims it to be. This is both an art and a science, and the best authenticators are part detective, part historian, and part scientist.

Here's how top-tier authentication works:

- Signatures - Experts compare handwriting, ink flow, stroke patterns, and even the age of the ink or pen used. They'll analyze it against known exemplars (verified examples) of that person's signature.

- Game-used items - Jerseys, bats, gloves, and shoes are inspected for wear patterns, tagging, stitching, material, and sometimes even DNA (yes, sweat or blood traces). Some authentications even involve photo-matching, lining up marks or creases in a jersey with known photos from a game.

- Cards and printed memorabilia - Authentication here involves checking the printing method, paper stock, cut lines, edges, centering, and possible forgeries. Modern cards may have embedded serial numbers or holograms that can be traced.

In recent years, we've seen authenticators using forensic tools such as UV light, microscopic analysis, and digital databases to back up their calls. That's how serious this business has gotten.

Even if something looks legit, always verify. Just because someone says "it came from a private signing" doesn't mean it did. Reputable dealers and auction houses rely on independent, third-party authentication. That's the standard. And if the item hasn't been looked at by a top-tier authenticator? Walk away or get it checked before putting your money on the table.

Table 6: Top Authenticators in the Game

CATEGORY	PRIMARY AUTHENTICATORS	NOTES / STRENGTHS
Sports memorabilia	PSA/DNA, JSA, Beckett (BAS/BGS), SGC, MEARS, Fanatics Authentic, Steiner Sports, UDA, Topps, CGC	PSA and Beckett lead in cards; JSA and BAS for signatures; MEARS dominates in game-used gear; Fanatics & Steiner for team provenance.
Entertainment memorabilia	JSA, Beckett (BAS), MAB, Schwartz Sports, PSA/DNA	Focused on autographs and signed memorabilia (e.g., movie scripts, posters, celebrity photos).
Pop Culture memorabilia	CGC, JSA, Beckett, PSA/DNA, MAB	CGC is top for comics and collectibles like Pokémon; Beckett/PSA/JSA certify signed items like toys, video games, music memorabilia.
History & Political memorabilia	PSA/DNA, JSA, Beckett	High-trust authentication needed for presidential signatures, documents, and culturally important artifacts.

Sources: Company websites and published authentication standards from PSA/DNA, Beckett Authentication Services (BAS/BGS), JSA, CGC, MEARS, Fanatics Authentic, Steiner Sports, Schwartz Sports, MAB Celebrity Services, and UDA. Data compiled and verified as of 2025.

Remember, authenticity is the bedrock of value. Without it, you're gambling. With it? You're investing.

The Dark Side of Memorabilia Collecting (Why Authenticate?)

Let's not sugarcoat it- where there's money, there are scammers. And with memorabilia, the stakes are high. Fraudsters are out there trying to pass off fakes, doctor items, or manipulate the market. If you are keen, you'll see it all - slick forgeries, shady COAs (Certificates of Authenticity), even stolen goods being flipped through back channels. These are some of the biggest frauds regarding memorabilia:

Table 7: Biggest Fraudsters and Items in Memorabilia

PERPET-RATOR (S)	CATE-GORY	ITEM(S) INVOLVED	YEAR (S)	DESCRIPTION
Overtime Promotions & Diamond Legends	Sports	Over 1,100 forged Jason Kelce autographed items	2025	Forged NFL memorabilia worth ~$200,000, allegedly authenticated by Beckett; three people charged.
Wolfgang & Helene Beltracchi *(Plate 5.1)*	Art	Fake paintings are attributed to Max Ernst, Campendonk, etc.	1970s–2010	Created and sold forged paintings with fake provenance, defrauding collectors of millions.
Knoedler Gallery	Art	Forged works are attributed to Pollock, Rothko, etc.	1990s–2000s	One of the biggest scandals in art; ~40 forged pieces sold for $80 million by a major NYC gallery.

Mehrdad Sadigh *(Plate 5.2)*	Antiquities	Fake Mesopotamian, Byzantine, and other ancient artifacts	1980s–2021	Ran a long-term forgery business in NYC; used tools to age modern fakes and issued fake certificates.
Unknown dealers (multiple cases)	Pop Culture	Fake Elvis Presley hair	1990s	Hair sold as Elvis's was later proven to be fake through DNA testing; widely circulated among collectors.
Konrad Kujau *(Plate 5.3)*	Historical/ Political	"Hitler Diaries"	1983	Forged diaries of Adolf Hitler published in *Stern* magazine; exposed through forensic ink analysis.
Charles Dawson (Piltdown hoax)	Historical/ Scientific	"Piltdown Man" fossil	1912 (exposed 1953)	Falsified fossil presented as an evolutionary link between apes and humans; exposed as a deliberate composite of human and ape bones.

Sources: Compiled from public legal records, news reports from The New York Times, The Guardian, ESPN & Smithsonian Magazine. Case details current as of 2025.

If you want to stay in this game- and win- you've got to learn how to spot the red flags. The most common types of memorabilia fraud include:

1. Forged autographs

Probably the #1 scam in the memorabilia space. With the right pen, lighting, and practice, a scammer can fake a signature that looks decent to the untrained eye. They'll even pair it with a knockoff COA from a no-name "authenticator" they created themselves.

2. Fake game-used items

Slapping some dirt on a jersey doesn't make it game-used. Fraudsters have been known to alter retail items to mimic actual in-game wear by adding stains, stretching fabric, even faking tagging or numbering. Without photo-matching or team-issued documentation, it's guesswork.

3. Reprints passed off as originals

Especially with vintage cards, tickets, and posters. Some sellers "forget" to mention it's a reprint or reproduction; others deliberately alter reprints to look old-aging paper by trimming edges, or fading colors.

4. Tampered trading cards

Cards that have been trimmed (cut to improve centering), pressed, or even doctored with color touch-ups to cover flaws. Once altered, they're no longer considered authentic by graders, and definitely not investment-grade.

5. Bogus provenance stories

"This was handed to my grandfather by Muhammad Ali." Maybe it was. But if there's no documentation or third-party validation, it's just a story. And stories don't sell, proof does.

Red Flags to Watch For

- Too good to be true pricing – If a $2,000 autograph is listed for $300, *ask why*.

- Vague or missing COAs – If the certificate isn't from PSA/DNA, JSA, Beckett, or another legit outfit, be skeptical.

- Pressure to buy quickly – Scammers often push fast sales to avoid scrutiny.
- Private listings with no track record – Always check the seller's history, reviews, and transaction record.
- Inconsistent details – If the story changes, or if the seller can't answer basic questions about the item-walk.

The best way to be safe is to buy from reputable dealers and auction houses. If you're dealing with a random seller online, do your homework (more on this in Chapter 4) and get a second opinion – even if an item has a COA, you can (and should) run it by another expert if you have doubts.

Verify serial numbers and LOAs. Most authenticators have databases where you can look up certification numbers to confirm the item and its description. You can also ask for photo-matching, especially with game-used gear. If it can be matched to an exact moment in time, it adds both credibility and value.

And of course, do everything you can to know the market. The more educated you are, the harder you are to scam. Knowledge is your first line of defense. Once you've satisfied these conditions, if something feels off, it probably is. Trust your gut, trust the process, and always trust the experts.

Always remember that protecting your collection isn't just about physical security or insurance (discussed in the next section) - it's also about playing the market wisely. The best collectors don't just buy what looks cool, they buy smart. Protection also includes:

- Market Research & Timing

Know when to buy, and when to hold. Understand market trends by staying informed about shifts in demand, which can affect the value of certain items. Some pieces, especially those tied to celebrities or athletes, may lose value once the individual's fame diminishes.

Timing is everything. Prices for rookie cards can spike with a breakout season, then cool off just as fast. The same goes for pop culture items tied to movies, music, or milestone anniversaries.

Diversify your collection. Instead of concentrating on a single type of memorabilia, consider spreading your investment across different items or niches to reduce exposure to individual market fluctuations.

Avoid market speculation. While certain items can be highly lucrative, chasing hype rarely ends well. Be cautious of trends driven by social media or influencer buzz, do your own due diligence before buying into the hype.

Pro tip: Track auction data, not just retail prices. Public auction results from platforms like Goldin, Heritage, or SCP Auctions are one of the best indicators of true market value.

- Liquidity Considerations

Know your exit strategy. Understand how easy (or difficult) it will be to liquidate an asset. The market for rare sports memorabilia can be less liquid than other investments like stocks or bonds, so be prepared for long holding periods.

Utilize auction houses and brokers. If you need to sell, work with reputable auction houses lor specialized brokers who can help find the right buyers. Each has its strengths depending on the type and value of your item- some are better for million-dollar game-worn jerseys, others for vintage card sets.

Understand commission structures and timelines. Auctions often charge both seller and buyer premiums, and payout can take weeks or even months after a sale.

- Risk of Counterfeiting

Work with reputable dealers. Establish relationships with known and respected memorabilia dealers who can guide you toward authentic items and help avoid forgeries.

Research item history. Be diligent in researching the item's past sales and any claims made about its authenticity. Always ask for certificates of authenticity (COAs) but remember that COAs themselves can be faked.

Use third-party authentication services. High-value items should be verified through multiple sources when possible.

Trust, but verify. Even vintage pieces. Old doesn't always mean authentic, especially in a market where counterfeits go back decades.

- Economic Downturns & Inflation

While memorabilia can be a great hedge during times of economic instability, it is still important to balance your portfolio with other asset types, like stocks, bonds, or real estate, to prevent exposure to a single risk.

Monitor inflation. Inflation can affect the value of physical assets, so keeping an eye on broader economic trends and adjusting your investment strategy accordingly is vital.

Collectibles can be recession-resilient, but not recession-proof. Some segments (like iconic sports cards or blue-chip art) may hold up during downturns, while niche or speculative markets may fall hard.

Store-of-value matters. Items with cultural or historical significance -Babe Ruth cards, Muhammad Ali trunks, first appearance comics- often perform better over time than trend-driven pieces.

Storage, Preservation, and Insurance

Once you've spent time and money on your collection, you need to protect it like you would any valuable asset.

1. Storage and preservation

Store graded cards in temperature-controlled environments. Use proper cases or graded card boxes. Keep raw cards in top loaders or magnetic holders and don't stack them without protection.

Game-worn jerseys, signed balls, bats and helmets all need custom cases. Keep them out of direct sunlight, UV light will fade autographs and damage materials over time.

Paper items such as tickets, programs, and photos need acid-free sleeves. Avoid basements and attics where moisture or heat can do long-term damage. Handle documents and artifacts with gloves. Use archival framing and matting. For metal items or flags, consult a conservator if they're fragile.

For costumes or props, display mannequins should be custom-fit and padded. Store textiles flat if possible, and away from moisture or pests.

Table 8: Memorabilia Storage Options

STORAGE TYPE	PROS	CONS	BEST FOR
In-Home Storage	Direct access, personalized display	Risk of environmental damage, theft, or loss	Daily access, aesthetic display
Bank Safety Deposit Box	High security, protected from disasters	Limited access hours, size restrictions	Small high-value items like cards, coins

Third-Party Storage Facility	Climate-controlled, expert handling	Monthly costs, restricted access	Large or valuable items needing care
Vendor Storage (e.g., auction houses, grading companies)	Professional handling, insurance usually included	May be temporary, access based on terms	Items waiting to be sold or graded

Pro tip: Document everything. Take high-quality photos. Save your purchase receipts. Record provenance if applicable. If you ever need to resell or file an insurance claim, you'll be glad you did.

2. Insurance

Ask yourself: If your collection disappeared tomorrow, could you replace it? If the answer is no, insure it. Be sure to get your pieces appraised regularly and use a specialty insurer that understands collectibles. A collection without insurance is just one flood or fire away from being a tragedy.

Most homeowners' policies don't adequately cover high-value collectibles. Talk to an agent about a collectibles rider or a separate fine art policy, it's usually affordable and well worth the peace of mind.

Table 9: Collectibles Insurance Providers

PROVIDER	BASED IN	SPECIALTIES	KEY FEATURES
Collectibles Insurance Services (CIS)	Westminster, Maryland	Sports memorabilia, comics, pop culture items	No appraisal needed under $25K, low deductibles, monthly value increases

Chubb	Warren, New Jersey	High-net-worth collections, fine art, rare collectibles	Global coverage, no deductibles, 150% agreed value payout, auto 90-day coverage
Berkley Asset Protection	New York,	Corporate and personal collectibles, fine art	Includes legal defense, restoration protection, risk management support
American Collectors Insurance	Cherry Hill, New Jersey	Collector vehicles, general collectibles	Inflation guard, automatic new item coverage, founded by collectors
AXA Art Insurance	Paris, France	Fine art collectibles, antiques	Global presence, multilingual support, flexible worldwide transit coverage
Hiscox	London, UK	High-value collectibles, art, jewelry	Customizable policies, international protection, digital inventory tools
Zurich Private Clients	Zurich, Switzerland	Ultra-high-net-worth items worldwide	Tailored insurance, disaster recovery plans, concierge claims handling

To narrow down your insurance options, ask yourself these three key questions:

1. What country are you based in (or where is the collection stored)?

   This determines which providers operate in your area and what coverage regulations apply.

2. What's the rough value of the collection? (e.g., under $10K, $10K–$100K, or over $100K).

   This affects your premium, deductible options, and whether an appraisal is required.

3. What type of memorabilia do you own? Is it primarily:

   - Trading cards (e.g., Pokémon, sports cards)?
   - Autographed items?
   - Comic books?
   - Other types of memorabilia?

Different insurers specialize in different categories, so matching your collection type to their expertise can save money and hassle. As a rule, here is what to look for in a collectibles policy:

- Agreed value coverage (vs. market value)
- Worldwide transit coverage
- Storage requirements (some require safes or vaults)
- Appraisal requirements for high-value items
- No deductible (in certain specialized policies)

Understanding Grading and Certification

If authenticity is the foundation of value, grading is the multiplier. It's what turns a cool card into an investment-grade asset. And if you're serious about collectibles you have to understand how grading works, who the key players are, and why the difference of half a point can mean the difference of tens of thousands of dollars. Items graded as PSA 10s that wouldn't sniff five figures as PSA 8s have sold for six figures. That's how powerful grading is. Let's break it down.

At its core, grading is about *standardization*. You're taking a collectible, having it evaluated by a third-party expert, and assigning it a numerical score (or qualitative assessment) that tells the world:

- Is this real?
- What kind of condition is it in?
- How does it compare to others out there?
- And most importantly: *what's it worth*?

Grading provides trust, confidence, and liquidity. It lets two people who've never met agree on the value of an item, and that's what drives a healthy market.

Subgrades are used by some authenticators like BGS and CGC's to show you what went into the final score. They break it down into:

- Corners
- Edges
- Surface
- Centering

If you're looking at two cards with the same grade, subgrades can tell you which one's actually better and which one deserves the premium. For example, Aa BGS 9.5 with three 9.5s and one 10 is more desirable than one with three 9s and one 10. That nuance can mean thousands of dollars.

Market Impact & Ranking of Grading Companies

Different authentication companies have a greater impact on valuation. When it comes to trading card grading and authentication, the industry has a few major players. The "ranking" among them can depend on factors like reputation, resale value, turnaround time, grading consistency, and cost, but here's a general tiered breakdown based on current industry perception: (Appendix 5 has a personal guide you can use to make the best choice for your collection)

Table 10: Grading Companies Ranked by Market Impact

GRADING COMPANY	TIER	PROS	CONS	BEST FOR
PSA (Professional Sports Authenticator)	Tier 1	Highest resale value, widely recognized and trusted, large population report	Higher cost, slower turnaround during peak demand	Sports cards, Pokémon, Vintage & modern memorabilia
BGS (Beckett Grading Services)	Tier 1	Subgrades provided, strong sports card reputation	Slightly lower resale than PSA, service delays	High-end modern sports cards, autographed cards
SGC (Sportscard Guaranty Corporation)	Tier 2	Fast turnaround, consistent grading, strong with vintage	Lower resale value for modern cards	Vintage cards (especially pre-war), sports cards
CGC (Certified Guaranty Company – Cards)	Tier 2	Comic grading credibility, fast service, clean slab design	Newer in card grading, resale still developing	Pokémon, Trading card games, Comic collectors
HGA (Hybrid Grading Approach)	Tier 3	Custom label options, AI-assisted grading	Inconsistent resale, Mixed reviews on accuracy	Personal collections, Display purposes
ACE, GMA, Others	Tier 3	Cheaper, quick turnaround	Lower resale value and market trust	Budget-conscious collectors, quick flips

Choosing the right grader matters, because the same card in different holders can have dramatically different market values. Whether you're collecting, flipping, or investing, understanding the grading ecosystem is essential to making smart decisions.

The Certification Process

Here's how the certification process typically works:

1. Submission

You choose your grading company, fill out the form, pay the fee (based on service level or card value), and send the item in.

2. Authentication

The first step is verifying it's real. This is especially important for autographs, vintage cards and artwork.

3. Condition evaluation

Trained experts (and in some cases, machines) examine every detail under magnification, proper lighting, and sometimes forensic tools.

4. Grading assignment

The item is scored, and in some cases, subgrades are assigned.

5. Encapsulation

Your item is sealed in a tamper-proof, sonically welded holder called a "slab." This preserves condition and confirms its grade and certification.

6. Certification number

Each item is given a unique serial number which you can look up in the grading company's online database. This adds traceability and trust.

If you're holding potential high-value memorabilia: grade it. Don't guess. Don't delay. A raw item might look nice, but a slabbed PSA 10 is a liquid asset. That's what investors are chasing. Grading isn't just a process, it's a passport. It lets your item travel through the hobby with credibility, value, and respect.

Rarity, Condition and Market Demand

Once you've locked down authenticity and dodged the fraudsters, you've got to ask the million-dollar question: What makes this item valuable?

The answer usually comes down to a powerful trifecta-rarity, condition, and market demand. These three elements are the fuel behind record-breaking sales, bidding wars, and the kind of heat that lights up auction night.

Rarity - Scarcity Creates Desire

Collectors crave what they can't have, that's human nature, and in the memorabilia world, it translates directly into dollars. The rarer the item, the more intense the competition. It's why a Honus Wagner T206 commands millions, and why game-worn gear from one-off moments gets snatched up in seconds.

But not all rarity is created equal.

- True rarity - This is when there are only a handful of something- maybe one, maybe ten. Think of 1-of-1 printing plates, championship-worn gear, or prototype items never released to the public. A Babe Ruth 1919 game-worn jersey fetched $4.4 million at auction in 2012, not just because it's a game-used jersey but because it's one of very few surviving from that era.

- Artificial rarity - This is where modern card companies limit print runs- like a /25 (only 25 copies/ pieces) or /10 (0nly 10), creating exclusivity. It's a powerful marketing tool and collectors go crazy for it. LeBron James 2003-04 Upper Deck Exquisite Collection Rookie Patch Auto /23 (*Plate 5.4*) sold for over $2 million in 2021 due to its limited print run, despite many other LeBron James rookie cards being more widely available.

- Contextual rarity - The item might not be rare in existence, but it becomes rare in context. For example, a LeBron James jersey is great, but the jersey he wore during his NBA debut. That's a different league. The Michael Jordan 1984-85 rookie jersey (worn during his first season with the Chicago Bulls) fetched $10.1 million in 2022 because it is tied to a historic moment in NBA history.

Bottom line: rarity adds gravity and makes people pay attention. And when the right story meets real scarcity? You've got magic.

Condition

Rarity gets buyers in the door; condition closes the deal.

We're talking centering, corners, surface, edges, wear, creasing, fading- you name it. For cards, it's why a PSA 10 rookie can go for 10x the price of a PSA 8. That difference is because of the condition.

And it's not just for cards. The condition of any type of memorabilia matters. Jerseys with heavy wear and strong photo-match potential? That's good condition in game-used. A signed photo with bold ink and zero smudges? That's premium. A ticket stub that survived decades without fading or tears? That's value.

Here's how the conditions play out:

- Cards – Graded on a 1-10 scale by PSA, BGS, or SGC. A half-point bump can mean thousands of dollars. A PSA 10 Michael Jordan 1986 Fleer Rookie Card sold for $738,000 in 2021, while the same card in a PSA 8 grade sold for around $40,000- that's a 700% difference in value purely due to condition.

- Autographs – Sharpness of the signature, no fading, no personalization ("To Dave") unless it's a personal connection to the buyer.

- Game-used gear – You want proof of action. Too clean? It might be retail. Look for wear, sweat stains, dirt, scuffs- those tell a story.

- Vintage items – Patina and light wear can add character, but damage subtracts value fast. It's a fine line.

One thing to always keep in mind with memorabilia - grade it, preserve it, protect it. You don't buy a Ferrari and leave it outside in the rain, the same goes for high-end collectibles.

Market Demand

Here's where it gets fun- and unpredictable.

Demand is where emotion, culture, and timing collide. It's where you need to spot the gems. For that, you need expertise and research. It's a lot like investing in a company; you wouldn't blindly put your money into a business that you didn't research, so you shouldn't do that for memorabilia either.

Often, items that sat quietly for years sell after something happens. A documentary drops, a Hall of Fame induction is announced, or a major headline brings someone back into the spotlight and suddenly, an item is hot. And when an item's hot, it flies. Jordan memorabilia exploded during and after his last game. A jersey that might've sold for $75k could sell for $300k. As sad as it is, major life events impact value too. When Kobe passed, the entire market surged with love and nostalgia and his memorabilia was hot. At the same time, pop culture crossovers will affect demand. A rapper mentions a vintage jersey in a song; a Netflix doc covers a baseball scandal and boom- suddenly everyone wants in.

It's also about who's buying. Wealthy collectors, hedge funds, athletes, and entertainers are getting in the game. They're not just fans- they're investors. And when high-net-worth buyers enter the space, prices follow.

If you want to know if something's going to appreciate over time, ask yourself:

- Is it genuinely rare?
- Is it in top condition (or has a compelling "worn" story)?
- Will this item be remembered long-term or is it a short-term fad?
- Is there real demand, now or soon?

If you've got all four? You're holding a rocket. And in this business, rockets don't sit still- they launch.

Putting It All Together

So, you've got a piece of memorabilia in your hands. The question on your mind- and every collector's mind -is simple:

"What's this worth?"

Now that you've walked through the pillars- authenticity, provenance, rarity, condition, and market demand- you're ready to put the puzzle together. Because the truth is, value doesn't come from one thing-it comes from the combination.

Here's how someone at an auction house like Goldin may look at value when evaluating a piece:

Verified Authenticity + Strong Provenance + Real Rarity + Top Condition + Hot Market Demand = High Value

If one piece of that equation is missing, the value drops. But when all five align; that's when the records break.

Case Study 1: 1986 Fleer Michael Jordan Rookie Card

In January 2021, a pair of 1986-87 Fleer Michael Jordan Rookie Cards were sold for a record-setting $738,000 each through Goldin Auctions. This is how it did in the value equation.

- Authenticity – Verified and graded by PSA.
- Provenance – Clear chain of ownership, certified since the '90s.
- Rarity – Not ultra-rare in raw form, but there are only a few hundred PSA 10s in the world.
- Condition – PSA 10 Gem Mint. Flawless.
- Market Demand – Off the charts, especially after "The Last Dance."

The same card in PSA 8, would have sold for around $10–15K. The condition alone created a multiplier effect.

Case Study 2: Kurt Cobain's MTV Unplugged Guitar

In 2020, the 1959 Martin D-18E guitar played by Kurt Cobain during Nirvana's 1993 *MTV Unplugged* session sold at auction for $6 million, setting a world record for a guitar.

- Authenticity - Verified, with supporting documentation and serial numbers.
- Provenance - Owned by Cobain, played in a widely recognized performance; verified through multiple sources including family and MTV.

- Rarity - One of a kind; this exact guitar was central to a cultural milestone.

- Condition - Used but preserved, with wear consistent with its public performance.

- Market Demand - Huge interest from both music fans and cultural investors, especially posthumously.

This case shows how crossover appeal - music, nostalgia, and 1990s cultural memory -can drive extreme value, even for a visibly used item.

Case Study 3: George Washington Signed Letter (1775)

A handwritten letter signed by George Washington from the early days of the American Revolutionary War sold for over $1.2 million in 2022 at Christie's.

- Authenticity - Fully authenticated with chain of custody, historical verification, and handwriting analysis.

- Provenance - Traced from historical archives to private collections; documented continuously.

- Rarity - Few such letters survive from this pivotal year, especially in good condition and with a full signature.

- Condition - Excellent for its age with just minimal fading and legible script.

- Market Demand - Exceptionally high due to the figure involved, the date, and renewed interest during periods of U.S. political introspection.

Here, the intrinsic historic value and national symbolism made this a prime long-term asset for institutional and private collectors alike.

Some items are meant for short-term flips, others for long-term holds. Knowing which is which can define your return.

In a hype cycle- like a breakout rookie season, viral documentary, or a record-breaking performance- prices can spike. Smart collectors ride the wave and sell into strength. Jeremy Lin memorabilia soared during "Linsanity," but cooled fast. Such memorabilia would have been short term by this strategy.

Long-term value, on the other hand, builds over decades. These are the assets tied to sustained greatness or cultural milestones- think Kobe Bryant's final game jersey, or a first-print copy of *Super Mario Bros.* The more iconic the figure or moment, the more stable the growth curve.

Even so, it is a balancing act.

- If you have a rare item but in poor condition, value takes a hit.
- A common item in mint condition may still have value, but it's capped.
- If you have a 1-of-1, perfectly graded item connected to a cultural moment, you're holding a rocket.

That's what makes this industry so exciting- it's never just about the object. It's about the story behind the object, the moment it represents, and the audience ready to chase it.

- If you're sitting on something and wondering what it's worth, here's a quick checklist:
- Is it authenticated? If not- get it done.
- Is there documented provenance? Any proof helps.
- How rare is it? Google it. Search auction comps. Check population reports.
- What's the condition? Be honest. Flaws matter.
- Is there demand? Is the athlete or artist relevant? Is there a resurgence in the market?

Is it a short-term pop or a long-term hold? Short-term - Riding a current wave? Sell strategically. Long-term - Legendary figure? Historic moment? Hold and protect.

And finally: What's the story? Because story sells. That's not just business, that's human nature.

If you've got an item that checks the boxes, treat it like the asset it is. Grade it, insure it, protect it, and when the time is right? The market will speak.

A Brief History of Collectibles

KEY INSIGHTS

- Successful collectors define their goals early - whether driven by passion, profit, or both. Your intent determines your strategy.

- Treat memorabilia like a financial asset. Create a budget, plan for hidden costs (insurance, grading, storage), and stick to a tiered investment strategy.

- Roll profits into stronger, rarer, or more culturally significant pieces. Aim to consolidate value over time - not just accumulate volume.

- Keep cash in hand. The right piece - the "grail" - can appear anytime. Flexibility is key to leveling up.

- Maintain a living ledger. Value your collection often, especially after key market events. Data-backed decisions drive stronger returns.

Whether it's a signed Beatles setlist, an Abraham Lincoln campaign flag (*Plate 6.1*), or a mint-condition 1977 Luke Skywalker figure (*Plate 6.2*), memorabilia speak to people and connects us to the past. But to build a meaningful, valuable collection- one that lasts- you need more than passion. You need a plan.

The collectible market, like any other, rises, falls, and evolves, and the collectors who thrive are the ones who treat their collection like a business and have a clear understanding of what they want out of the experience. They don't just buy, they build. This chapter will show you how you do it too.

Setting Goals – Passion Vs. Profit

When it comes to memorabilia, your "why" is everything.

Are you in this to own history? Maybe you're tracking down every major item from your favorite team's championship run. Or maybe you grew up watching *Star Wars* and want original props from the trilogy. That's passion.

Or are you in this to build long-term value? You're treating memorabilia like a blue-chip asset. You want scarce, authenticated, investment-grade pieces with cultural or historical gravity that will appreciate over time. That's profit.

Both are valid, but your approach has to match your intent.

If you're a passion collector, maybe you're hunting down every card from the '86 Fleer basketball set because that's what lit you up as a kid. Or maybe you're building a museum-quality lineup of game-used memorabilia from your favorite team. In this case, emotion drives decisions more than ROI, and that's okay- just understand that your returns may be emotional, not financial.

If you're collecting for profit, your mindset needs to be sharper. You're buying on comps. You're looking at population reports, tracking market trends, and understanding timing. You're thinking about liquidity. You're not buying what you love, you're buying what others will want in 3, 5, 10 years.

Smart collectors find a balance. Passion fuels your commitment, profit keeps you disciplined. Know where you stand and revisit that question as your collection evolves.

Budgeting and Financial Planning

Let me give it to you straight: The fastest way to crash and burn in this industry is to *overspend without a plan*. Just like any financial asset, your collection deserves a budget. Too many people get swept up in a bidding war, swipe the credit card, and regret it two weeks later when the rent's due.

Here's how to stay grounded:

1. Set an annual memorabilia budget

Think of it like a portfolio allocation. How much of your disposable income can you *responsibly* dedicate to collectibles? 5%? 10%? Do the math. Use '5% of your portfolio for memorabilia as your benchmark.

Keep in mind that this % covers all the costs associated with collecting, not just purchasing the memorabilia, but also storage, insurance, authentication and any other hidden costs. As a rule of thumb, expect to spend an additional *20%–30% on top of the item's purchase price* to cover all supporting costs. Here's a rough breakdown to guide your expectations:

- Buyer's Premium (Auctions): 10%–25%
- Sales Tax / VAT: 5%–20%
- Authentication / Grading: 1%–10%
- Appraisal Fee: Flat or 1%–5%
- Insurance: 1%–2% annually
- Storage / Display: 2%–5%
- Restoration / Conservation (if needed): 5%–15%
- Shipping & Handling: 1%–5%

If you plan to collect across categories, break your budget down. You could have 50% of your collectible allocation go to sports memorabilia, 25% to entertainment memorabilia, 15% to pop culture and 10% to historical memorabilia. Play around with the percentages to get a combination that is right for you. Focus on what you are good at and enjoy investing in and then put a small amount aside for speculation.

Tweak based on your goals, but don't buy blindly. Just because something looks cool or starts trending, doesn't mean it fits your strategy. Disciplined budgeting and cost awareness separate savvy collectors from impulsive spenders.

2. Use tiers

Not every piece needs to be a grail; tiers will help you create a value ladder. Tier 1 could include your core pieces – the big-ticket items you'll hold long term. Tier 2 includes speculative plays, items with potential for flipping, and tier 3 includes the fun purchases; the things that just make you happy.

3. Document everything

Build a spreadsheet. You need a ledger. In the ledger, include purchase price, current value (based on comps), and notes. Not only does this keep you organized, but it helps with insurance and eventual sales. Provenance documentation supports authenticity and passage of clear legal title, proving the value of your piece and bettering your chances for a positive ROI.

If you can, digitize the important financial documents, appraisal and condition reports, and any other literature pertaining to your memorabilia. While at it, add important contacts so that you have the details of your appraisers, lawyers, sellers, conservators and any other relevant party in one place. Keep them updated. That way, you will never have to stress about getting valuable information in an emergency. For pieces that need maintenance, each time it is done, record what happened, who did the maintenance, and how much it cost. Schedule a reminder for upcoming maintenance so that you never forget.

4. Value Often

When it comes to memorabilia, the market never sits still. What something's worth today might be dramatically different six months from now. That's why you need to value your items often. Not once a year, not when you feel like it. Often.

A collectible isn't just a keepsake - it's a living asset. And like any asset, its value fluctuates with the market. The passing of a sports legend can send signed gear soaring overnight, a documentary can reignite global interest in a player, or a reboot can make a forgotten franchise red-hot again. If you're not watching the market, you're falling behind.

Every six months minimum is a great benchmark for staying current. And if there's a major event - a death, a record-breaking sale, or a viral moment - reassess your item immediately. You don't wait when you're holding an asset that could appreciate 20–50% overnight. You act.

You should also be sure to value your items before the big milestones; before you sell, before you insure, before you hand something down or split assets. Whether it's estate planning or divorce, an undervalued collection creates problems. It is extremely easy to leave a lot of money on the table because of an unchecked value.

For your heavy hitters - the six-figure items, the 1-of-1s - get a professional appraisal every two years. Use someone accredited, who knows your category, not just any appraiser. Use a sports card expert for cards or a pop culture specialist for movie memorabilia. Trust matters.

In between formal appraisals, use the data. You want a portfolio built on numbers, not guesses. Look at sold listings on eBay, not asking prices. Study the results from Goldin, Heritage, RR Auction and relevant auction houses. Whatever your niche, there's a reliable source. Know it. Watch it. Use it.

And never forget, the condition is value. The same item in different conditions can have a 10 times price difference; take care of your items. Grade them if you think they'll score high and re-grade if the market moves.

5. Reinvest wisely

The best collections are built with intent, not impulse. Flipping a piece for a profit is only half the game. What do you do after that sale? That's what separates the casual collectors from the ones building generational collections.

When you move an item and come out ahead, you have three smart options. You can reinvest it back into your collection fund, fold it into your general finances, or go all-in on your next grail item.

None of these are wrong, but discipline here is everything.

The best collections aren't just a pile of cool stuff, they're intentional. They tell a story. Whether it's rookie cards from every NBA MVP, autographs from every U.S. president, or screen-worn pieces from 80s action films, the elite collections have purpose, and that purpose guides every reinvestment.

Let's break it down.

- Roll profits into stronger pieces

Say you've sold a signed Derek Jeter ball (*Plate 6.3*) for $2,000. That's a win. Now what? Maybe you step up to a photo-matched game-used Jeter jersey for $15K. This is how collections evolve- trading 10 "nice" items for one "elite" one. Quality over quantity always wins at auction.

- Level up your niche

If you're deep in vintage Hollywood memorabilia, and you just sold a James Dean signed check, don't pivot into baseball cards on a whim. Stay in your lane, but elevate. Go after that screen-worn *Rebel Without a Cause* jacket or a Marilyn Monroe signed contract- pieces with provenance and gravity.

- Keep some liquidity

Not every dollar from a sale has to go back into collectibles. Maybe you peel off 20–30% for life expenses, savings, or just holding cash for the right opportunity. Being over leveraged in collectibles can backfire if the market shifts.

- Target the "grail" with intent

Every great collector has a white whale. Maybe it's the ticket stub from Jordan's debut, or one of the moon-flown Apollo 11 patches. When you spot that grail- be ready. Having dry powder in reserve- or stacking wins from smaller flips- gives you the firepower to strike when it hits the block.

Here's what your budget table might look like: (Appendix 6 provides you with an editable Google Worksheet you can customize).

CATEGORY	DETAILS	AMOUNT ($)	NOTES
Initial Investment			
Purchase Cost (Item 1)	Example: Signed Baseball (Mickey Mantle)	3000	Cost of items including shipping/fees
Purchase Cost (Item 2)	Example: Basketball Jersey (LeBron James)	5000	Cost of items including shipping/fees
Purchase Cost (Item 3)	Example: Vintage Card (Pele)	10000	Cost of items including shipping/fees
Total Initial Investment		**18000**	
Maintenance Costs			
Insurance	Estimated insurance cost for items (per year)	500	

Storage Costs	Climate-controlled storage fees (per year)	300	
Grading & Authentication Fees	Authentication, grading services (per item)	100	Example cost for authentication service
Total Maintenance Costs		**900**	
Projected Return Value			
Estimated Value (Item 1)	After 3–5 years of market growth	7000	Based on market data, potential appreciation
Estimated Value (Item 2)	After 3–5 years of market growth	8000	Based on market data, potential appreciation
Estimated Value (Item 3)	After 3–5 years of market growth	15000	Based on market data, potential appreciation
Total Projected Return		**30000**	
Profit Estimate (after costs)			
Total Projected Return		30000	Projected value after 3–5 years
Minus Total Investment		-18000	
Minus Maintenance Costs (5 years)	900/year x 5 years	-4500	Total maintenance cost over 5 years
Estimated Profit		6600	

Figure 6: Memorabilia Investment Sample Budget Table

Note: The initial investment is the total amount you spend buying the memorabilia items including shipping and fees. The maintenance costs include annual insurance and grading costs.

You can customize your budget into tiers and allocate assets for diverse types of memorabilia.

- **Tier 1 Buys** - High-value, long-term investment pieces that are rare, historically significant, or have high market demand. These are items you expect to appreciate significantly in value over time. They could include signed jerseys from top athletes, vintage cards (T206 Honus Wagner), or game-worn memorabilia from iconic moments. Typically, 60-70% of your total budget could be allocated to Tier 1 buys if you're a serious collector/investor.

- **Tier 2 Buys** - Mid-range items with moderate value potential. These may not be as rare or historically significant, but they still offer solid growth potential. They could be signed baseballs from up-and-coming players, limited edition prints, or lesser known but still valuable sports items. Around 30-40% of your total budget can be allocated to Tier 2 buys.

Imagine investing $30,000 into memorabilia- not just as a passion project, but as a strategic, tiered portfolio. Like any alternative asset class, collectibles benefit from diversification, risk management, and a clear understanding of market dynamics. The examples below show how an investor might allocate capital across different types of memorabilia by tier- from core blue-chip items to more speculative or "fun" plays- and how to manage a collectibles budget as part of a broader financial strategy.

The first table outlines a tier-based investment model, allocating capital based on potential return, historical performance, and market liquidity. The second example zooms out, showing how a $5,000 collectibles budget (5% of a $100,000 income) might be distributed across different memorabilia categories, tiers, and supporting costs like insurance, storage, and maintenance.

Whether you're managing $5K or $500K, the goal is the same: treat memorabilia like the asset class it is, with structure, discipline, and long-term vision.

Asset Allocation by Type of Memorabilia

This section will break down how you might allocate your budget across different types of memorabilia, based on your goals and risk tolerance. Bear in mind that you can adjust budget allocation categories based on your priorities:

Table 11: Sample Tiered Budget Breakdown (With Asset Allocation)

CATEGORY	DETAILS	TIER 1 BUDGET	TIER 2 BUDGET	TOTAL BUDGET
Total Investment		**$20,000**	**$10,000**	**$30,000**
Autographed Memorabilia	High-value autographed jerseys, shoes	$10,000	$5,000	$15,000
Vintage Cards	Iconic rookie cards, rare baseball cards	$5,000	$2,000	$7,000
Game-Worn Gear	Jerseys worn in famous games	$3,000	$1,500	$4,500
Sports Artwork/Other Collectibles	Limited edition prints, event tickets	$2,000	$1,500	$3,500
Maintenance & Storage	Insurance, storage, grading fees	$500/ year (10% of total budget)	$500/ year (10% of total budget)	$1,000/ year

Based on the type of asset, you can expect the following returns:

- 5-15% per year for autographed memorabilia
- 10-25% per year for vintage cards, with significant spikes for rare auctions
- 10-20% per year for game worn gear
- 5-10% per year for artwork and collectibles especially limited-edition pieces

Figure 7: Tier-Based Asset Allocation Table

CATEGORY	% OF BUD-GET	AMO-UNT ($)	TIER 1: CORE	TIER 2: SPEC-ULATIVE	TIER 3: FUN	STORAGE & INSURANCE
Total Income	100000					
Collectibles Budget	5%	5000				
Sports Memorabilia	50%	2500	1500	700	300	200
Entertainment	25%	1250	700	300	250	100
Pop Culture	15%	750	400	200	150	50
Historical	10%	500	300	100	100	30
Totals	100%	5000	2900	1300	800	380

Buying and Selling Memorabilia

KEY INSIGHTS

- Auction houses - Negotiate fees, focus on net proceeds, set smart reserves, and tell a compelling story.
- Dealers - Verify authenticity, start small, avoid shady sellers, and build trust.
- Private Sales - Lower fees but do your homework; use escrows for big buys.
- Online Platforms - Fast, global, and varied, but beware of fakes; always check ratings and recent sales.
- Local Venues - Great deals and rare finds; inspect carefully and negotiate face-to-face.

If you're in the memorabilia game just to make a quick buck, let me save you some time; this probably isn't the lane for you.

The memorabilia world isn't built on fast flips or flashy headlines even though those things do happen sometimes. It's built on passion, patience, and an understanding of value that goes deeper than price tags. Sure, you might stumble upon a hot item and ride the hype wave to a quick profit, but the real collectors, the real investors? They're playing a long game.

This isn't like stocks or crypto. You're not trading numbers on a screen, you're trading stories. You're holding history in your hands. Whether it's a $50 card of a prospect you believe in, or a $5 million jersey worn by an all-time great, the fundamentals never change:

- Know your product - Understand what you're buying. Learn the difference between a base card and a parallel. Know the significance of a game-used bat versus a stadium giveaway. The more you know, the more confident you become-both as a buyer and a seller.

- Know your buyer - Are they a collector? A flipper? An investor? Each has a different mindset, and each values items differently. When you know who you're selling to, you can speak their language and close stronger deals.

- Know your timing - This one's key. People often leave tens of thousands on the table simply because they listed too early or waited too long. The calendar matters. Market cycles matter. Momentum matters. It's not just what you sell, it's when.

Let me tell you something I've learned again and again: The real money isn't always made on the sale, it's made when you buy right. If you don't know what something is worth, you can't spot the opportunity when it shows up. You'll either overpay and chase the market or undersell and regret it forever.

This is about intrinsic price.

Intrinsic price is the true, underlying value of an item based on its fundamentals-authenticity, rarity, condition, provenance, and cultural or historical significance. It's what the piece is really worth, independent of hype or market noise. Unlike the current market price, which can fluctuate with trends or short-term emotion, intrinsic price is rooted in long-term value.

But the intrinsic price isn't fixed. It moves with new information. A card that was worth $1,000 yesterday could be worth $5,000 today if it's photo-matched to a championship game, or if the athlete suddenly becomes a Hall of Famer. The reverse is also true; if a signature is exposed as fake, the value can collapse instantly.

Smart collectors and investors don't just react to prices, they understand what drives them. They evaluate comps, verify authenticity, assess market momentum, and track narratives. That's how you buy right, by knowing the intrinsic value before the auctioneer hits the gavel.

In this business, information is leverage. Whether you are buying or selling, knowledge is power. Enjoy acquiring it like you would if you were investing in any other market.

- Study the comps (comparative sales).
- Watch how auction trends shift.
- Build relationships- with dealers, collectors, and yes, auction houses.
- Learn to spot value not just in grades and signatures, but also in stories.

Because here's the truth: A card isn't just cardboard. A jersey isn't just fabric. These are relics of culture, of legacy, of moments that changed history forever. And when you treat them with that kind of respect- when you understand that history has value- you unlock a market that's bigger than any one trend.

That's what this chapter is about: how to navigate the buying and selling process the right way. Not with hype or guesswork but with strategy, knowledge, and that gut-level instinct you only get from being in the trenches. Whether you're just getting started or managing a seven-figure collection, this chapter is your playbook for transacting on your memorabilia. Remember that each platform has its own audience and advantages, so the choice often depends on the type of memorabilia being sold and the seller's/buyer's preferences.

Where to Buy or Sell Memorabilia

1. Auction Houses

Auction houses are the heartbeat of high-end memorabilia; nothing matches the energy of a major auction night. At an auction house, you'll find rare items you simply won't see elsewhere, and you get the following benefits:

- Global audience – You're not just selling to someone down the block, your buyer could be in Tokyo, Dubai, or sitting courtside in LA. Through an auction, you can sell to collectors, investors and even celebrities from all over the world.

- Authentication – Reputable houses will always vet every item in their catalogue, this ensures trust. In an auction house, credibility is baked in. Most reputable houses work with third-party graders like PSA, BGS, JSA, MEARS, etc.

- Maximized value – In an auction, competition drives prices up. There is a bidding war, and that works well for you as a seller.

In 2022, the Goldin house sold a 1997-98 Metal Universe PMG Green Michael Jordan card (*Plate 7.1*) for $915,000. There were only 10 in existence. The bidding was intense and drove the price up so that the final price shattered comps by a mile. That's the magic of a live auction; it is driven by market forces, so you can almost always guarantee that you get the best price.

There, you avoid the stress of haggling with a dealer who is much more adept at the game. Top auction houses will do all the work for you. You don't have to write descriptions or shoot photos or print beautiful catalogs. You simply ship your memorabilia, and they do the rest.

Pro tip for sellers: Be sure you know the auction calendar, timing matters. Drop that NFL item just before the Super Bowl or that LeBron piece before the Finals. The right timing can make or break your sale.

Pro tip for buyers: As a buyer, set a ceiling. It's easy to get emotional and overbid. Don't. Stick to your strategy and before the purchase, research past auction results. Sites like WorthPoint or the auction house's own archives are goldmines for comp data.

Here are the top auction houses in the world. Appendix 3 provides a longer list of the same alongside their official websites.

Table 12: Top Auctions in the World

AUCTION HOUSE	LOCATION	SPECIALTIES
Goldin Auctions	Runnemede, New Jersey, USA	Sports memorabilia, trading cards, pop culture collectibles
Heritage Auctions	Dallas, Texas, USA	Sports collectibles, comics, coins, fine art, historical memorabilia
Sotheby's	New York, London, Hong Kong	Fine art, luxury goods, rare collectibles (incl. sports and pop culture items)
Christie's	New York, London, Hong Kong	Fine art, watches, rare memorabilia, historical items

What To Know Before You Hand Over Your Memorabilia to an Auction House

If you're going to consign a piece- whether it's a single big-ticket item or a full collection- you need to understand the rules of the game. The right auction house can get you top dollar, no question. But the details in the fine print? That's where your margin lives or dies.

Here's what I tell people all the time based on real-world deals, not guesswork:

- Understand the commission structure

The commission is the cut the house takes from your final sale price. Standard is around 20%, but it's absolutely negotiable, especially if you've got a standout item or a high-value collection. With a sealed case of 1986 Fleer or a game used jersey for example, you could pay 0% commission because your item drives attention, traffic, and bidders. That's leverage.

It's also worth remembering that auction houses also make their money on the buyer's premium, sometimes up to 20–21% tacked onto the winning bid. That's called "the juice." So even if they give you a great deal on the seller's side, they're still in a good spot.

- Don't obsess over the cut, focus on the net

Too many people nickel-and-dime a commission rate and then walk away from a house that could've pulled $20K more for the same item. Don't trip over pennies on your way to dollars. Your goal isn't to pay the lowest fee, it's to walk away with the biggest check.

- Ask about authentication fees

Big houses usually work with PSA, JSA, MEARS, etc., and get better rates than you or I would on the open market.

Sometimes they'll eat the cost for you if the item is strong enough, other times, they'll pass it on quietly. An item with a $100 authentication fee that sells for a few hundred bucks can lose you money, so ask upfront.

- Watch for miscellaneous fees

Most major sports memorabilia houses play it straight- no hidden storage fees, no surprise insurance charges. But in the broader collectibles space it does happen. Make sure you get a breakdown in writing before you ship anything off.

- Set a realistic reserve or starting price

If you've got a premium item, protect it with a reserve. That's the floor- the minimum you're willing to accept. It keeps you from waking up to find your rare Ali glove went for half what it should have. But be reasonable, an unrealistic reserve just kills momentum.

- Go for prime-time placement

Every auction house has tiers. The headline auctions- the big, seasonal ones with all the marketing muscle- draw the heaviest traffic. That's where you want your marquee pieces. Some houses also run weekly or monthly sales, which are great for lower-tier inventory, but don't bury your million-dollar Mantle in a bargain bin.

- Be involved in the cataloging

This one's big. You know your item better than anyone, help write the listing. Suggest angles, facts, even emotional hooks. One detail can help your item smash expectations. You don't have to be a writer, just give them the story. The story is where value lives.

- Don't be a pain

Auction houses are often juggling dozens, sometimes even hundreds of consignors. When the auction opens, it's chaos.

Be respectful, be clear, and don't demand daily updates like your piece is the only one in the catalog. The best results come from long-term relationships, not one-and-done deals. Be the kind of consignor who people want to work with, and you'll be amazed how often that goodwill pays you back.

2. Dealers

A good dealer is worth their weight in gold. They've got access, experience, and often the inventory before it even hits the market. The best ones know the pulse of the market. But like any industry, there are bad actors, so do your homework. You know a dealer is good if there is:

- Transparency – The dealer needs to tell you the full story of the item you are interested in; provenance, condition, grading.

- Consistency – Their prices need to make sense in the current market.

- Network – A dealer is good if they can find what you are looking for, or if they can find the perfect buyer for the thing you're selling.

Forming relationships with solid dealers can lead to great off-market deals. Just remember, verify, authenticate, and always get paperwork. Watch out for unrealistic pricing, lack of authentication or pressure tactics.

Tips for engaging with dealers

- Do your research - Familiarize yourself with current market values and trends.

- Ask questions - Inquire about the item's history, condition, and any certificates of authenticity.

- Start small - Begin with less expensive items to build trust before making significant investments.

- Get everything in writing - Ensure all agreements, including authenticity guarantees and return policies, are documented.

Here are some well-known memorabilia dealers worldwide. You'll find a longer list in Appendix 3.

Table 13: Top Dealers in the World

DEALER NAME	LOCATION	SPECIALTY	WEBSITE
Exclusive Memorabilia	UK (Devon)	Signed sports memorabilia	https://www.exclusivememorabilia.com
Steiner Sports	USA (New York)	Authenticated sports memorabilia	https://www.sportsmemorabilia.com
Goldin	USA (New Jersey)	Premium trading cards and signed items	https://www.sportsmemorabilia.com

One downside of buying through dealers is that some dealers may mark up prices significantly, especially if they know a buyer is emotionally attached to a particular piece. Others may use high-pressure sales tactics to create urgency, or worse, pass off unverified items as genuine. That's why paperwork - especially Certificates of Authenticity (COAs) from top-tier authenticators - and documented provenance should always be non-negotiable.

So, where do you find these dealers?

- Official websites

The most direct route is to start with their official websites. Leading names like Exclusive Memorabilia, SportsMemorabilia.com, and Icons.com offer certified inventory across a range of categories. In the Middle East, outlets like Camel Comics and The Bootroom Collection provide premium sports and pop culture memorabilia, often tied to international franchises and limited-edition releases.

- Google/Apple maps

Outside of their websites, you can locate dealers through local searches on Google Maps or Apple Maps using queries like "signed sports memorabilia near me" or "pop culture collectibles (your city)."

- Specialty galleries

Specialty malls and galleries often house exclusive dealers. In Dubai, for example, stores like The Collect Room, Comicave, and Speedy Comics carry autographed items, vintage comics, and limited-run collectibles.

- Social media

Social media is another powerful tool. Many top-tier dealers consistently post new inventory, announce private signings, and promote exclusive drops on Instagram, X, and Facebook. Following dealer accounts not only gives you timely access, but also allows you to observe how engaged and responsive they are with their communities - often a good indicator of credibility.

- Online communities

Finally, join collector forums and groups. Online spaces like Reddit's r/AutographCollectors or private Facebook groups offer insider perspectives, real-time reviews, and alerts on dealer scams. These communities can be your first line of defense and your most valuable allies when navigating the dealer landscape.

A good dealer can be the difference between a world-class acquisition and a costly mistake. Find one who knows their craft, honors the details, and treats collecting with the seriousness it deserves.

3. Private Sales

Private sales aren't just for celebrities and billionaires. They're for savvy collectors who want discretion, speed, and a tighter margin on fees. These sales can be brokered by dealers, auction house reps, or directly between collectors, and give you the following benefits:

- Lower fees – In a private sale, you do not need to pay the auction commission, so you make more money. A well-structured private deal often allows the seller to net more and the buyer to pay less, creating a true win-win scenario.

- Speed – If both parties agree, a deal can happen in hours. This makes them ideal for time sensitive acquisitions or opportunistic purchases when market dynamics shift quickly.

- Privacy – Private sales keep major items off the public radar. Items won't be listed publicly, there's no searchable auction result, and the exchange remains between trusted parties.

Be sure to do your homework if you go down this route. In a private sale, due diligence is 100% on you. You have no safety net, so you better know what you are buying before you spend your money.

Tips for Navigating Private Sales Wisely

- Verify authentication - Always request Certificates of Authenticity (COAs) from a reputable source, depending on the category.

- Request provenance - Ask for a clear paper trail. Who owned it before? How did they acquire it? Even in private deals, documentation is a must.

- Benchmark pricing - Use auction results to ensure the item is priced fairly for its rarity, condition, and market relevance.

- Use escrow services - For high-value deals, consider using an escrow service to hold funds until the item is delivered and authenticated.

- Build relationships first - Try to establish trust before transacting. That may involve small purchases or meeting through a collector forum or mutual connection.

Several online platforms now facilitate private sales with varying degrees of exclusivity:

- House of Assets – A luxury collectibles marketplace for ultrahigh-net-worth individuals

- Back to the Past Collectibles – Known for vintage toys, comics, and memorabilia with private selling services.

Contact reputable private dealers directly to explore their inventory. You can also follow them on social media and attend their private signing events. Forums like Net54Baseball, are also great to see private opportunities and secure invite-only showcases. The following table has a list of some of the top private dealers you can consult.

Table 14: Top Private Memorabilia Dealers

NAME	SPECIALTY	PLATFORM / WEBSITE	NOTABLE DETAILS
Ken Goldin	High-end sports memorabilia, trading cards	https://www.goldin.co/	Brokered over $1.3B in sales; Netflix's *King of Collectibles*

Loïc Gouzer	Fine art and rare collectibles	n/a	Former Christie's chairman; invitation-only private sales via mobile app
Paul Fraser	Historical documents, autographs, pop culture	https://www.paulfrasercollectibles.com	One of the largest, rare collectibles dealers globally
Bruce Hershenson	Vintage movie posters	https://www.emovieposter.com	Over $5M in annual poster sales; established private marketplace
Memory Lane Inc.	Sports memorabilia, vintage cards	https://www.memorylaneinc.com	Offers brokering and private sale services for high-value sports items

Table 15: Notable Memorabilia Collectors & Their Collections

NAME	SPECIALTY	COLLECTION HIGHLIGHTS
Gary Cypres	Sports Memorabilia	Recognized as the world's largest private sports memorabilia collection, featuring items from over a century of sports history.
Steve Sansweet	Star Wars Memorabilia	Holds the Guinness World Record for the largest Star Wars memorabilia collection, with over 500,000 items at Rancho Obi-Wan.

Leo S. Ullman	Nolan Ryan Memorabilia	Owner of the most extensive Nolan Ryan collection, with 15,000+ items including rare artifacts like custom boots and portraits.
Andrew Longoria	Selena Quintanilla Memorabilia	Holds the Guinness World Record for the largest Selena memorabilia collection, totaling 1,308 items as of June 2024.
Candy Spelling	Antique Dolls	Amassed a vast antique doll collection since 1980, reflecting deep emotional and historical interest.
Bob Crotty	Chicago Cubs Memorabilia	Holds a remarkable collection of vintage Cubs artifacts and memorabilia related to legendary players.
Brad Horn	Baseball Memorabilia	Former Baseball Hall of Fame spokesperson with a deep collection of historical baseball items.

Source: VICE, Wikipedia, MySA, Financial Times. All details verified as of 2025.

4. Online platforms and marketplaces

The rise of platforms like eBay, PWCC, MySlabs, Alt, and Whatnot has opened the gates to global buyers and sellers. It's 24/7, 365. It is worth making a distinction between online marketplaces, digital-first auction platforms, and traditional auction houses. Online marketplaces & platforms (e.g., eBay, MySlabs, Whatnot) are open, peer-to-peer or app-based platforms where anyone can list or buy memorabilia. Many are optimized for mobile, some with live streaming.

Traditional auction houses (e.g., Heritage, Sotheby's, Christie's) are curated, often high-end institutions offering premium memorabilia through cataloged sales. They usually include formal appraisals, provenance research, and full-service support.

Online platforms and marketplaces provide:

- Accessibility – You don't need a million-dollar collection to get started.
- Speed – You can buy and sell items in minutes.
- Variety – On these platforms, you get everything from a $5 rookie card to six figure pieces.

Online platforms and marketplaces come with their own challenges. There are some risks, such as counterfeits and shill bidding, inconsistent grading or emotional buying. Always check a seller's feedback or rating and choose only graded and authenticated items (you can use filters so that you only see graded items) and watch comps throughout the sale. Always compare with recent sold listings and not just the asking prices, and whenever possible, message sellers for more details or photos, especially for raw cards or anything ungraded.

Here's a quick look at the major platforms, what they do best, and what to expect:

Table 16: Online Platforms, Marketplaces and Apps

PLATFORM	TYPE	BEST FOR	FEES	KEY FEATURES
eBay	Online Market-place	Mass-market collectibles, auctions	13-15%	Huge user base, authenticity guarantee for high-end items
Amazon	Online Market-place	New and licensed mem-orabilia	Varies by item	Good for mass-produced and signed merch

Etsy	Online Market-place	Vintage, framed items, art-based collectibles	Varies by item	Niche memorabilia, signed photos, custom display pieces
Sports Memorabilia. com	Specialized Website	Jerseys, auto-graphs, display-ready items	Varies	Licensed by major leagues & authenticators (Fanatics, Steiner, PSA)
PWCC Marketplace	Specialized Website	Vaulting, premium card auctions	Varies, low fees for listing	Real-time market analytics, premium card focus
Alt	Mobile/Web App	Data-driven, graded cards, vaulting	Sub-scription/ Trading Fees	Portfolio tracking, investment-grade cards
MySlabs	Mobile/Web App	Graded cards, sealed wax, authenti-cated mem-orabilia	1% Seller & Buyer Fee	Peer-to-peer marketplace, low fees, collector-focused
Whatnot	Mobile App	Live-streaming auctions	Varies by auction	Fast-paced, impulse buying, great for quick sales

Table 17: Social Media Platforms

PLATFORM	BEST FOR	RISKS	KEY FEATURES
Facebook Marketplace	Local deals, no fees	No protection, authentication risks	Local, direct transactions, no shipping costs
Instagram	Flash sales, direct engagement with collectors	Risk of counterfeit items	Dealer pages, flash sales, easy access
Reddit	Active trading hubs (r/sportsmemorabilia, r/baseballcards)	Lack of official authentication, scams	Community-driven, self-policing, escrow suggestions

As a rule of thumb, use PayPal Goods & Services or an escrow whenever you can with these platforms.

The best online sellers build a brand. They show high-quality photos, they write detailed descriptions, they engage. And the best buyers do their homework. They compare comps, ask questions, and negotiate with respect.

This space moves fast. But if you learn the platforms, understand the risks, and play it smart, it can be one of the most profitable and exciting ways to build your collection, or sell it.

Remember: it's not just about selling fast, it's about selling smart.

5. Local Venues

As digital platforms dominate the industry, it's easy to forget that some of the best deals still happen in person. Behind card shop counters. Across folding tables at hotel ballrooms. In booths at conventions. Even in local auction halls where a little-known jersey might go unnoticed until the right eye sees it. Don't sleep on local venues. If you know what to look for, they can be absolute goldmines.

The human element of in-person collecting when using local venues adds real value. You can ask questions, inspect items, and negotiate directly, often leading to better deals or bundled discounts. Talking with experienced collectors and dealers can also help you gain critical insight into grading, pricing, and authentication.

The cherry on top is that many sellers at local shows or shops don't list online, so you'll find raw, underpriced, or rare items that you won't see on eBay or major platforms. These spaces foster relationships that can lead to long-term partnerships, trade opportunities, or early access to inventory.

The downside is that items aren't always graded or authenticated, so spotting fakes or flaws requires a sharp eye. Also, since many sellers prefer cash, there's little buyer protection compared to online platforms. Not only that, but most sales are final. You need to be confident before you buy.

For local venue options, you can check:

- Hobby and memorabilia shops

Brick-and-mortar stores still move serious inventory. Many buy, sell, and trade cards, autographs, jerseys, and even sealed wax. You'll often find raw cards here, which is great if you know how to grade by eye. Some shop owners are old-school collectors with deep knowledge and even deeper back rooms. Ask the right questions and you might get shown something not on display.

- Flea markets and collectible shows

They may sound low-budget, but don't underestimate them. You'll find tables with everything from bulk commons to vintage treasures, often priced below eBay. These shows attract dealers who don't sell online, so inventory can be fresh and under-the-radar. Always bring a loupe and flashlight-

you might be the first to really inspect that raw memorabilia item.

- Local auctions

Smaller regional auction houses sometimes run dedicated auctions, or tuck memorabilia into estate or collectibles sales. The competition is usually lower, and the pricing is often well below market. You'll need to do your homework though.

- Conventions

Conventions are hubs for every kind of memorabilia imaginable. Whether you're into sports, pop culture, comic books, historical items, or entertainment collectibles, conventions can be a good place to source or sell items. These events bring together serious collectors, hobby newcomers, dealers, authenticators, auction houses, and even celebrities or athletes connected to the pieces we chase.

You'll find everything from vintage jerseys and signed balls, to original Star Wars props, presidential letters, or movie-used memorabilia, all under one roof.

Big shows like the National Sports Collectors Convention (NSCC) cater to sports memorabilia, while events like Comic-Con, Fan Expo, or more niche conventions like autograph fests or pop culture expos, have booming markets for signed photos, movie-worn costumes, and unique collectibles.

In these conventions, you get to deal directly with sellers, collectors, and even representatives from major auction houses or authenticators. The cherry on top is that these places are great for networking. They are where partnerships start, deals get made, and information flows freely. You can negotiate in person, bundle items, ask questions, get provenance info, or make on-the-spot trades. Whether you're buying, selling, or just learning, conventions are some of the most exciting and educational places to be in the memorabilia world. And you never know who you'll meet or what you'll walk away with.

- Appraisal and consignment services

Some shops and local businesses offer consignment services-they'll help appraise, market, and sell your high-value items. These can be helpful for first-time sellers who don't want to deal with logistics, especially for older collections or inherited items. Just be sure to understand their fee structure before signing anything.

Negotiation and Pricing Strategies

Deals are made or lost in negotiation. Whether you're at a show, online, or talking one-on-one, know your numbers. Don't just price based on emotion or what you "feel" something's worth.

For Buyers

- Do your homework - Look up recent sales. Use tools like Card Ladder, Market Movers, or auction archives.
- Don't be afraid to walk - Sometimes the best deal is the one you don't make.
- Bundle when possible - If someone has multiple pieces you want, there's often wiggle room.

First-Time Buyer's Checklist

The memorabilia market is exciting (especially in online markets), but it moves fast and not everyone's playing fair. Use this checklist to avoid fakes, overpaying, or buyer's remorse.

Research the Item

- Check recent sales of the same item or close comps.
- If graded, verify the cert on PSA/BGS/SGC websites.
- Understand the pop report- rarity drives value.

Inspect the Listing

- Look at all photos and make sure to zoom in on corners, edges, surfaces.
- Check for cracks or damage on slabs.
- Make sure the description matches the photos.

Vet the Seller

- Check feedback and reviews (eBay, MySlabs, Whatnot ratings).
- Ask for references or "vouches" on social media.
- If on Facebook or Instagram, only pay via PayPal Goods & Services unless you fully trust the seller.

Buy Smart

- Stick to your budget- don't get emotional.
- Use filters to only view graded/authenticated listings.
- Ask questions-"Can you send more photos?" is always fair game.

Close with Confidence

- Make sure the seller ships with tracking and insurance.
- Confirm shipping timelines, especially on high-dollar items.
- If you're vaulting (Alt, PWCC), confirm that the asset will be transferred directly.

For Sellers

- Know the market - Price too high, and you sit on your item forever, price too low, and you leave money on the table.
- Know your floor - Decide beforehand what your lowest number is.
- Build value - Great photography, detailed descriptions, and proof of authenticity make a difference.

- Negotiation is expected - Always price with a cushion for wiggle room.

- Factor in timing - Selling a Chiefs item in February after a Super Bowl win? You'll get a premium.

- Use grade population data- A PSA 10 with a pop of 15 is going to move differently than one with a pop of 2,000.

First-Time Seller's Checklist

Whether you're listing a single card or a prized piece of game-used memorabilia, this list will keep you from leaving money on the table-or making rookie mistakes.

- Know what you're selling

- Is it graded? Know the grade and population.

- Is it authenticated? Have proper certs (PSA, JSA, Beckett, MEARS).

- If raw, check the condition under good lighting-corners, centering, edges, surface.

Price with precision

- Look at recent comps, not just what others are *asking*.

- Use tools like eBay sold listings, Card Ladder, Market Movers, or 130point.com.

- If you are auctioning, know the starting bid or set a reasonable reserve.

Presentation is everything

- Take clear, well-lit photos, front and back.

- Show close-ups of autographs, serial numbers, flaws, or certs.

- Write an accurate, honest description- include athlete/celebrity if relevant, year, brand, serial number, authentication info.

Platform Prep

- Choose the right platform (eBay for volume, PWCC for slabs, MySlabs for low fees, Whatnot for live action, etc.).
- Know the fees involved and how they affect your bottom line.
- Offer secure shipping with tracking and insurance for high-value items.

Be strategic

- Time your sale - Sell NFL items in January, NBA in June, etc.
- Promote it on Instagram, Reddit, or collector groups to build buzz.
- Respond quickly to questions to build trust with buyers.

The memorabilia market is stronger- and more exciting-than it's ever been. But this isn't the Wild West anymore. Knowledge, strategy, and relationships win here. Whether you're flipping a $500 card or selling a $5 million jersey, how you buy and sell determines your long-term success.

Imagine that you have a PSA 9 1986 Fleer Jordan rookie and want top dollar, but the market is soft. What do you do? Rather than list it cold, you can bundle it with three other Jordan inserts from the 90s, create a themed lot, and auction it as a "Jordan Investor Collection." Chances are it will outperform expectations. You should always play to your strengths to get the best out of your memorabilia.

Remember: every item has a story. And in this business, the story is often just as valuable as the signature.

Plate 4.1 – Patek Philippe watch
Source: *Patek Philippe*

Plate 4.2 – T206 Honus Wagner Card
Source: *Wikipedia*

Plate 5.1 – H. Beltracchi posing in photo to fake provenance.
Source: *Polizei*

Plate 5.2 – Mehrdad Sadigh forged antiquities collection
Source: *NY Times*

Plate 5.3 – Forged Hitler Diaries
Source: *Britannica*

Plate 5.4 – LeBron James Exquisite rookie patch
Source: *Sportscar investor*

Plate 6.1 – Abraham Lincoln Campaign flag
Source: *Wikipedia*

Plate 6.2 – 1977 Luke Skywalker
Source: *Wikipedia*

Plate 6.3 – Signed Derek Jeter Ball
Source: *Steiner Sports*

Part III:
THE FUTURE OF MEMORABILIA

There was a time when collecting was all about the thrill. You didn't need spreadsheets or cap tables, just a sharp eye, a good gut, and maybe a little luck. Maybe you found a Jackie Robinson rookie card at a garage sale for five bucks. Maybe your grandfather passed down a signed Mantle ball. These weren't "assets" in the way Wall Street defines them, they were stories, memories. They were personal.

But over the past decade, something fundamental has changed. What began as a hobbyist's game has evolved into a global investment class. This isn't a side hustle anymore - it's serious business.

The global memorabilia and collectibles market is estimated at over $294 billion as at 2025, and it's projected to keep growing at a CAGR of 5.5% in the years leading to 2030, fueled by demand for authenticity, nostalgia, and scarcity. Within that, sports memorabilia alone is forecasted to exceed $26 billion annually, and the pop culture and entertainment memorabilia segments aren't far behind. And we're only scratching the surface.

We've entered a new era - one where vintage trading cards, game-worn jerseys, autographed sneakers, first-edition comics, and sealed Pokémon boxes are being targeted by hedge funds, family offices, and high-net-worth investors. Platforms like Goldin, PWCC, Alt, and Collectable are backed by venture capital. Institutional money is flowing in. Banks and wealth managers are starting to view collectibles as a viable allocation alongside stocks, real estate, and art.

Why? Because the fundamentals are starting to look familiar: limited supply, growing demand, and a cultural tailwind that's impossible to ignore. These aren't just nostalgic trinkets; they're appreciating, diversifiable assets with asymmetric upside.

The rise of institutional-grade platforms is changing how collectors interact with memorabilia. Secure vaulting, fractional ownership, on-chain provenance, and seamless global access are becoming standard features. This infrastructure appeals not only to hedge funds and family offices seeking diversification but also to younger generations - Gen Z and Millennials - who want to invest in the cultural artifacts that shaped their identities, blending emotional connection with financial strategy.

This cultural asset class is no longer niche or underground; it's stepping onto the global stage with institutional rigor and technological innovation. The fusion of finance, emotion, and identity is reshaping the market, and the stories behind the assets - the legends, the moments, the meaning - have never been more valuable.

And make no mistake, what we are seeing is just the tip of the iceberg.

The third part of the book will dive into where this market is heading, from fractionalization and tokenization to new tech platforms, regulatory changes, and a shift in generational wealth. We'll explore how collectors, investors, and institutions are converging, and what it means for anyone holding or hunting serious pieces of history.

The future of memorabilia isn't coming. It's already here.

The Institutional Shift

For decades, collectibles were seen as the domain of die-hard fans, hobbyists, and weekend warriors. But today, the world is catching up to something a few people have known all along; that these items have real, measurable value. And now they're earning their place in institutional portfolios right alongside stocks, bonds, and real estate.

We're witnessing a major paradigm shift. What was once considered a fringe 'asset' class is now drawing attention from wealth managers, family offices, hedge funds, and alternative asset platforms. The reason is simple: collectibles are scarce, culturally significant, and often uncorrelated with traditional financial markets, making them an increasingly attractive hedge in volatile times.

Trading cards, sports memorabilia, comic books, vintage toys, original artwork, sneakers - these are no longer just stored in closets and display cases. They're being underwritten, insured, fractionalized, and in many cases, securitized for broader investment exposure.

High profile moves like Blackstone's backing of Collectors (PSA), Alt- one of the world's leading authentication and grading companies- letting people trade graded cards as if they were stocks and funds, and syndicates acquiring items like a 2009 Mike Trout rookie card or a pristine Action Comics #1 not as trophies, but as appreciating assets show you that collecting memorabilia is becoming a portfolio strategy.

As institutional capital pours in, a new player is taking center stage: the custodian. Custodians are third-party companies that physically secure, store, and manage high-value assets on behalf of investors or collectors. Think of them as the equivalent of a bank vault for collectibles, with the added layers of authentication, insurance, auditing, and often digital access.

Firms like PWCC Vault, Alt, Collectors Vault (by PSA), and Goldin are leading this custodial shift. These platforms ensure that the item's condition is preserved, documentation is traceable, and that ownership can change hands without the asset ever needing to leave the facility, removing friction and adding legitimacy.

Why does this matter? Because of the independence they provide. Custodians are not necessarily buyers or sellers; they're neutral third parties. That neutrality creates transparency and trust, both essential for institutions that require compliance-ready records, verified ownership, and insurance-backed storage. It also allows for seamless integration into digital marketplaces, fractional platforms, and future tokenization strategies.

In short, custodians are infrastructure. And infrastructure is what turns a niche hobby into a scalable investment class.

The collectible markets are still young compared to equities or real estate. But what we're seeing now isn't just hype; it's structure, it's systems. It's a foundation for what comes next.

Historically, collectibles had a few things working against them from an institutional perspective- valuation uncertainty, authentication challenges, and illiquidity. But that's changing. Fast.

- Valuation

In the early days of collecting, valuation was art, not science. One person's $10,000 card was another's $1,000 gamble. But as prices rise and the stakes grow higher, the industry is maturing. Companies today are collecting massive datasets from auctions, marketplaces, and private sales. Price indices now track assets the same way the S&P tracks equities.

Collectors and investors alike now have tools for comp analysis, volatility tracking, and portfolio modeling. We're seeing market-making behaviors, with buy-sell spreads tightening and arbitrage opportunities being actively exploited. The availability of high-frequency data has legitimized collectibles in the eyes of institutional investors.

For example, Fanatics- a prominent U.S. sports merchandising group- is significantly expanding its presence in the trading card market. Led by CEO Michael Rubin, the company plans to generate nearly $3 billion in revenue from its collectibles division by 2026. This expansion includes acquiring exclusive rights to English Premier League cards and opening its first trading card store in London.

Similarly, Rally is a platform that allows users to buy and sell equity shares in collectible assets. Founded in 2016 and headquartered in New York, Rally has expanded its offerings to include over 300 assets across various categories such as art, wine, watches, sports collectibles, and first-edition books. Each asset is registered with the SEC as security, providing a level of regulatory oversight that appeals to institutional investors.

- Authentication and grading

Expectedly, institutional investors don't play in opaque markets. They need trust, and that's exactly what the ecosystem has been building.

Grading companies have become the gatekeepers of authenticity. What they provide aren't just opinions, they're industry standards that determine value. Provenance, chain of custody, and condition reports have become as critical as the asset itself. For the highest-value items, we now see chain-of-custody documentation, forensic photo-matching, and blockchain tokenization to ensure provenance is immutable.

That way, you're not just buying a card or a pair of sneakers-you're buying into a verified, trusted asset.

- Liquidity and exit markets

For years, the biggest knock against collectibles as an asset class was liquidity. You might have a million-dollar item, but what if nobody was willing to buy it? What if you needed to wait six months for an auction window? What if the market turned?

That's changing fast.

Live marketplaces now facilitate 24/7 bidding, instant offers, and even secondary markets for fractional shares. Some platforms are exploring automated market-making mechanisms and OTC-style block trades for high-end collectors and institutions. Liquidity is no longer an afterthought- it's becoming a feature.

As this ecosystem matures, we're seeing investors treat collectibles like alternative assets in a diversified portfolio. In some cases, they're even being used as collateral for loans and margin credit. That's not speculation- that's a sign of infrastructure.

And there's another layer to all this which can't be ignored.

Traditional assets don't carry the same emotional or cultural resonance. A stock can't make you feel the way a signed Tom Brady jersey or a first-print Charizard can. Collectibles tap into cultural relevance, generational identity, and emotional resonance. That gives them staying power. These aren't just stores of value; they store cultural history.

Institutional players are realizing this. For Gen Z and Millennials who grew up with Pokémon, Jordan, Kobe, and LeBron, these assets mean something. They're not just trophies. They're touchpoints of identity, and when identity meets scarcity, value follows.

It is no surprise that we are seeing early signs of structured funds built around collectible baskets. Private equity firms are entering the space. There are discussions of multi-family offices allocating to collectibles as part of their alternatives strategy. There are even conversations among insurance companies and endowments exploring long-duration exposure to high-grade memorabilia.

From hobby to asset class. From basement to boardroom.

This transformation didn't happen overnight, but it's happening fast, and the same passion that fueled this market in its earliest days is now driving its professionalization. The world is waking up to memorabilia as an asset class in its own right.

Democratizing Access

In the past, ownership was binary: you either had the item, or you didn't. That kept the high-end of the market exclusive; reserved for ultrahigh-net-worth individuals who could spend $2 million on a bottle of wine or $5 million on a a-list autographed script.

Today, the collectibles market is undergoing a seismic transformation, driven by the convergence of technology, blockchain, and a new generation of investors. Where access to high-value memorabilia was once limited to the wealthy elite or seasoned collectors with deep networks, platforms like Rally, Collectable, Courtyard.io, and Dibbs are changing the game, opening the vault, so to speak, to everyone.

Now, these platforms have turned that model on its head. Through fractional ownership, investors can now buy shares in collectibles, just like shares in a company. You no longer need a seven-figure checkbook to participate. Instead, you can own a stake in a blue-chip collectible for ten, hundreds or thousands of dollars.

This has democratized access and enhanced liquidity-two critical ingredients for any asset class to go mainstream.

Fractionalization allows high-value assets to be split into hundreds or thousands of shares. These shares can then be offered to the public at affordable price points, making it possible for everyday investors, including younger collectors and retail participants, to own a piece of iconic cultural history.

Take Rally, for example. They've offered fractional ownership in everything from a first-edition Harry Potter book signed by J.K. Rowling to a Lamborghini Countach. Collectable has brought fractional shares of sports memorabilia like a 1986 Fleer Michael Jordan rookie card PSA 10 to investors for under $50 a share. This is not just investing, it's cultural participation. This model dramatically expands the pool of potential investors. No longer is a $1 million bottle of whiskey locked away in a safe or auctioned to a single high-net-worth individual. Now, thousands of people can participate in its ownership, share in its appreciation, and engage with the collectible as a community.

What's powering this shift behind the scenes is tokenization - the representation of physical or digital assets as tokens on a blockchain. This adds a whole new layer of transparency, liquidity, and security to the collectibles market.

Courtyard.io, for instance, securely stores physical collectibles- like graded Pokémon cards- in vaults, and issues blockchain tokens that represent ownership. These tokens can be traded globally 24/7 without the need to physically move the item. Dibbs takes a similar approach, using blockchain to fractionalize and tokenize sports cards in real-time, enabling rapid and secure trading.

Tokenization isn't just a tech trend- it's a structural evolution. It ensures trust, because the blockchain provides a permanent, immutable record of ownership. It provides traceability, as every transaction is recorded and verified. And most importantly, it enhances global accessibility. Now, a collector in Singapore can co-own a rare LeBron James rookie card with an investor in New York or Berlin. Borders don't matter. What matters is passion, belief in the asset, and participation in a market that used to be exclusive.

These innovations are democratizing the collectibles space in a way we've never seen before. Investors who were previously priced out can now gain exposure to appreciating cultural assets, diversify their portfolios, and actively engage in an asset class that's as much emotional as it is financial.

The future of collectibles is no longer just in glass cases and auction houses, it's in vaults, on-chain, and in the hands of people who might never physically hold the item but will still take pride in owning a piece of history.

We're entering a new era- one where memorabilia is no longer just owned by the few, but experienced by the many.

International Appeal

The collectibles market is no longer just a domestic conversation - it's a global movement. What started in the United States with baseball cards and action figures has exploded into a multi-billion-dollar international phenomenon. As online platforms, digital vaults, and cultural trends transcend borders, we're witnessing a surge in demand from every corner of the globe.

North America remains the epicenter of traditional card culture. The dominance of the NBA, MLB, NFL, and NHL has long driven American collectors, but what's remarkable is how deeply this culture has now rooted itself abroad. The global popularity of stars like LeBron James, Shohei Ohtani, and Patrick Mahomes has turned rookie cards and game-worn gear into international investment assets.

Meanwhile, Japan has cultivated one of the most passionate and enduring collector bases, driven by the global obsession with Pokémon- a brand that, to this day, continues to produce some of the most sought-after and valuable cards in the market. In fact, a 1998 Pikachu Illustrator card, originally released exclusively in Japan in 2024, fetched over $5 million in private sales, illustrating the longevity and international pull of Japanese IP.

Europe is also quickly becoming a powerhouse in the global memorabilia space, fueled by the continent's deep-rooted love for football (soccer). Collectibles tied to UEFA Champions League stars like Kylian Mbappé, Erling Haaland, and Jude Bellingham are seeing meteoric rises in both value and demand. Add to that the rich legacy of World Cup legends like Pelé, Maradona, and Zidane, and you have a market steeped in history and ready to boom. Rookie stickers, Panini cards, and autographed gear from these icons are not just collectibles, they're investments and status symbols across Europe and the Middle East.

Markets like India, Brazil, and Southeast Asia are stepping into the spotlight with force.

- India is seeing growing demand for cricket memorabilia, especially items tied to national icons like Sachin Tendulkar, Virat Kohli, and MS Dhoni. As India's middle class grows and digital infrastructure improves, we're seeing more interest in auction platforms and tokenized ownership.

- In Brazil, there's rising interest not only in football legends like Ronaldinho and Neymar, but also in crossover content like anime cards and K-pop collectibles, both of which appeal to younger demographics.

- Across Southeast Asia, the surge of esports and anime fandoms is pushing collectibles related to games like *League of Legends*, *Valorant*, and shows like *One Piece* and *Attack on Titan* into the mainstream collecting space.

With platforms like Goldin, eBay Vault, and PWCC, international buyers can now access elite collectibles stored in secure U.S. vaults without the logistical headache of international shipping or customs. A collector in Dubai or Manila can bid in real time on a 1-of-1 Tom Brady card, win the auction, and have it safely stored, all without the item ever leaving the United States.

This model of digital vaulting and trading is not just about convenience, it's about scalability. It's what allows the memorabilia market to operate like a true financial market - borderless, secure, and transparent.

We're also witnessing the rise of a sort of 'cultural investing'. Gen Z and Millennials aren't just chasing ROI, they're investing in emotion, authenticity, and identity. Pop culture, nostalgia, and representation matter more than ever.

Whether it's a signed BTS album, a Steph Curry jersey, a Messi rookie sticker, or a vintage Yu-Gi-Oh! card, today's investors are saying, *"I want to own what I love."* This generation is redefining what value looks like, and it's not just about dollars.

Private Debt and Securitization

As the collectibles market continues to mature, we're heading toward another change: the emergence of private credit and securitization. Today, the top assets in this space - PSA 10 cards, game-worn jerseys, signed memorabilia, and graded comics - are already being recognized as stores of value. But soon, they'll become something even more powerful: financial instruments that can be borrowed against, lent on, and packaged into structured investment products.

In the near future, collectors won't need to sell grail items to access capital. Instead, they'll be able to borrow against their collectibles, just like you would with real estate or fine art, memorabilia items will serve as collateral for private loans. Firms like PWCC Capital and Lendary are already laying the groundwork, and we expect their models to evolve into full-fledged private lending platforms, offering:

- Collateralized loans to collectors, allowing them to tap into the value of their assets without relinquishing ownership.

- Yield-generating products for investors, who can lend capital secured by high-grade, insured collectibles held in secure vaults.

This will unlock tremendous liquidity for the market. Collectors will be able to grow their portfolios without forced sales, and investors will gain access to stable, asset-backed returns in a new corner of the alternative lending universe.

Where it gets even more exciting is the securitization of collectibles. Just as mortgage loans or art portfolios have been turned into structured investment products, we're on the cusp of seeing collectible-backed securities emerge.

Picture this:

- A bond-like instrument, backed by a curated basket of blue-chip sports cards.

- A thematic securitized offering consisting of all game-used memorabilia from 1990s NBA legends.

- Yield-generating products composed of vintage comic books, Pokémon first editions, or global football grails.

These products will be professionally underwritten, rated, and offered to institutional and accredited investors, providing predictable cash flow and exposure to a low correlation, culturally resonant asset class. Expect platforms to bundle fractional shares, loans, and vault-held inventory into investment-grade products that can be traded, syndicated, or even listed on secondary markets.

Of course, for all this to take hold, the foundation must be solid; and it's rapidly coming together. Advances in grading standards, blockchain-based provenance, digital vaulting, and insurance infrastructure will be the bedrock that gives institutional investors the confidence to participate on a scale.

Once those systems are fully integrated, we'll see collectibles treated not just as assets of passion, but as financial instruments with yield potential, liquidity, and institutional credibility.

The writing is on the wall: collectibles are on track to become a legitimate asset class within the global credit markets. What began in childhood bedrooms and auction houses is heading straight for the portfolios of hedge funds, private banks, and fixed-income strategists.

As I see it, we're not far off from a world where a graded Tom Brady rookie doesn't just live in a vault - it backs a bond. And for collectors, that means more flexibility. For investors, it means more opportunity. And for the market as a whole, it means the best is still to come.

Memorabilia Investment Funds

We can also expect another frontier for collectibles beyond vaults, platforms, or auctions - one that opens the door for everyday investors. As the market matures and investor sophistication grows, memorabilia-focused investment funds will become increasingly accessible to retail participants, allowing everyone to join in on this exciting asset class. Over the next few years, this democratization of collectibles investing will accelerate dramatically.

And not just casual plays by hobbyists. We're talking about structured funds with institutional backing, asset management strategies, and performance mandates. And why not? The collectibles market has shown explosive growth, with blue-chip assets demonstrating strong, often market-beating returns.

Several early movers have already laid the groundwork for how these funds may operate:

- Alt Fund is building a model around sports cards, sealed wax, and video games, combining cultural relevance with data-backed investment rigor. Their platform infrastructure is already providing real-time valuation tools and a trading ecosystem, paving the way for a scalable fund product.

- Myco is looking toward the future with tokenized, blockchain-native IP and collectibles, offering fractional access to everything from comic book rights to digital collectibles tied to music and entertainment. Their vision is a fully liquid, 24/7 investment market, built on the principles of Web3.

- HAGI-style indexes - modeled after the Historic Auto Group Index - are in development for graded trading cards and sports memorabilia, providing benchmark tools that could support ETF-like products or actively managed collectible funds. With standardized indexes, we'll see more institutions and retail investors able to track, measure, and allocate to this asset class.

- Iconic Collectors is creating a memorabilia fund that will be detailed in appendix 1.

As it is, collectibles preserve value during inflationary cycles and have a low correlation to equities and fixed income, making them great for diversification. It helps that they also resonate with the next generation of investors, Millennials and Gen Z don't just want exposure to traditional financial assets - they want their portfolios to reflect what they care about.

This broad generational alignment and the rise of user-friendly platforms are driving wealth managers, private banks, and fintech startups to design accessible memorabilia investment options for retail clients - not just for returns, but for relevance and emotional connection.

Consider this example: A PSA 10 Michael Jordan Fleer rookie card, which sold for around $50,000 in 2019, peaked at over $700,000 just a couple years later, in 2021. That's not just appreciation, that's outpacing equities, gold, and real estate over the same period. Now imagine a fund with 100 of those cards, properly insured, vaulted, and actively managed alongside other blue-chip assets like a Wayne Gretzky O-Pee-Chee rookie, a game-worn Messi jersey, or a sealed first-edition Pokémon booster box. That's not speculation - that's a diversified, retail-accessible investment strategy designed to unlock value for a wide range of collectors and investors alike.

Insurance, Vaulting and Trust Infrastructure

As collectibles evolve from personal passions into serious financial assets, the infrastructure supporting the market must evolve with them. For institutional capital, family offices, and global collectors to fully participate, the market needs one thing above all: trust - trust in the security, authenticity, valuation, and tradability of the assets.

We're now witnessing the rise of a robust trust infrastructure designed to give collectors and investors' confidence that their high-value memorabilia are not only safe, but also liquid and investable.

Leading insurance providers like Chubb, Hiscox, and AXA XL, have stepped in to underwrite collections with values ranging from five figures to eight and beyond. These aren't just hobby policies, -they're customized fine art-level coverage for assets like:

- PSA 10 sports cards
- Game-worn jerseys
- Signed championship equipment
- Original comic book issues
- Vintage Pokémon

Soon, you can expect to see insurance seamlessly integrated into digital marketplaces and vaulting platforms, so that from the moment of purchase to long-term storage, assets are covered, logged, and risk-managed without additional friction.

Not only that, but gone are the days of shoeboxes in closets. Today's -and tomorrow's- collectibles live in climate-controlled, secure vaults, with instant access to markets, insurance, and liquidity tools.

Vaulting services like the Goldin Vault, eBay Vault, PWCC Vault, and Courtyard.io are redefining what it means to "own" a collectible. Soon, owning a PSA 10 Steph Curry rookie or a 1st edition Harry Potter won't just mean holding it, it will mean digitally accessing it, trading it, borrowing against it, or fractionalizing it, all without moving the asset an inch.

These vaults provide:

- Secure, climate-controlled storage to preserve asset integrity.
- Integrated insurance coverage for peace of mind.
- Digital access to instant selling, trading, and fractionalization, eliminating the time, cost, and risk of shipping high-value items.
- Regulatory-compliant transparency for provenance and title.

Central to this trust infrastructure are custodians - independent third-parties that provide neutral, secure storage and management of collectibles. Custodians are unbiased gatekeepers, safeguarding assets on behalf of investors or collectors, ensuring authenticity and condition are maintained without conflict of interest. Their role enhances confidence by separating ownership from physical possession, creating a layer of independence critical for institutional involvement.

By removing the barriers traditionally tied to physical assets like shipping delays, customs complications, and ownership transfer paperwork, vaulting platforms operated by custodians enable borderless collecting and investing. A buyer in Edinburgh can acquire a LeBron rookie stored in the U.S. and immediately list a fractional share to buyers in London, Dubai, or São Paulo.

This trust infrastructure reduces capital friction, increases liquidity, and makes the collectibles market function more like a modern, regulated financial exchange. And that's exactly where we're headed.

Impact of Technology and AI

Technology, particularly artificial intelligence (AI), is rapidly revolutionizing the collectibles market in ways that were unimaginable just a few years ago. From the moment an item is authenticated to the moment it changes hands, AI is enhancing transparency, accuracy, and speed.

One of the most significant applications of AI is in authentication. Autographs, cards, jerseys, and other memorabilia are now being examined through AI-powered image recognition and pattern analysis tools. These systems can detect subtle inconsistencies or anomalies that might elude even the most experienced human experts. By automating the authentication process, AI reduces the risk of fraud and forgery, which historically has been a major challenge for collectors and investors alike. The technology doesn't replace expert judgment, but acts as a powerful assistant, flagging items for further human review and thereby increasing the overall reliability of certification.

Beyond authentication, AI is also transforming how collectibles are priced and valued. Traditional valuation often relied heavily on human expertise and comparative sales data, which could be limited and subjective. Today, machine learning models can analyze vast datasets including historical sale prices, market trends, social media chatter, and collector sentiment, in order to forecast future values and highlight emerging investment opportunities. This data-driven approach allows collectors and institutions to make smarter, more informed decisions, helping to navigate the market's volatility and spot potential "hidden gems" before they become widely recognized.

However, while AI brings remarkable benefits, it is not without its challenges. The technology's effectiveness hinges on the quality and completeness of data, which can vary significantly across categories. Niche markets or rare items with little sales history present difficulties for algorithmic analysis. Besides, AI-generated valuations and authentications still require human oversight to interpret the nuances that machines might miss. Experts remain essential to validate AI findings, manage exceptions, and maintain the trust of the collecting community.

Despite these hurdles, the integration of AI into the collectible's ecosystem is advancing steadily. Auction houses, grading companies, and online marketplaces are increasingly adopting AI tools to streamline operations and boost transparency. Soon, collectors can expect an environment where items are authenticated faster, pricing is more precise, and trading is smoother, all supported by intelligent technology that enhances, rather than replaces, human expertise.

AI is helping to elevate the collectibles market from a passion-driven hobby into a trusted, data-informed asset class. As technology continues to mature, it will unlock new levels of efficiency, accessibility, and security, paving the way for a truly modern, global collectibles economy. And alongside this evolution, new types of memorabilia are emerging, expanding the boundaries of what collecting means in the digital age.

Experience-based memorabilia are gaining traction, where value lies not just in physical objects but in unique moments and access. Collectors now prize items like VIP lanyards, backstage wristbands, or event-used seat stubs, authenticated and sometimes enhanced with blockchain verification. Video recordings of personal meet-and-greets or virtual reality tokens for exclusive performances transform intangible experiences into collectible assets. Imagine owning a signed NFT video of a meeting with a sports icon, or an augmented reality wristband commemorating a historic concert.

Similarly, social media artifacts are becoming prized collectibles. Screenshots of iconic tweets or viral posts minted as NFTs - such as Jack Dorsey's first tweet, which sold for $2.9 million - highlight how digital footprints of fame hold cultural and financial value. Viral moments, memes, live streams, and even deleted content recovered and authenticated by platforms, expand the realm of what is collectible. Owning the original TikTok that launched a celebrity career is now possible.

Video games and the metaverse introduce another frontier; in-game collectibles. Skins, weapons, characters tied to esports legends or major tournaments, limited-edition digital items signed by players or developers, and metaverse-native trophies function as the digital equivalents of autographs and memorabilia. For example, an exclusive Fortnite skin signed by a pro gamer and stored securely in a blockchain wallet blurs the line between virtual and real-world collectibles.

Audio-only memorabilia offers rare sound-based assets, such as voice notes, unreleased audio clips, first demos, or limited drops of podcast segments, all authenticated and tokenized. Imagine owning a private voice message from Tupac or a rare studio rehearsal by Prince - intangible yet deeply valued pieces of music history.

Finally, augmented reality (AR) memorabilia are redefining physical collectibles by embedding digital enhancements. Posters or jerseys that trigger AR animations, 3D holograms of athletes or musicians linked to signed merchandise, and smart memorabilia equipped with NFC chips or embedded sensors bring a new interactive dimension to ownership.

Together, these innovations mark the dawn of a collectibles market that embraces both tradition and technology. The future is not just about owning physical artifacts but engaging with culture, history, and identity in ways that were once unimaginable.

Final Thoughts

From Roman soldiers engraving victories on coins, and medieval pilgrims treasuring saintly relics, to tribal societies wearing carved totems of ancestors, humanity has always created and preserved reminders of meaning. Memorabilia is our collective resistance to forgetfulness.

It's why fans pay millions for a glove worn in a World Series, why families carefully frame war medals passed down through generations, and why digital natives now mint viral moments on blockchains. Each piece declares with quiet power:

"This happened. I was there. It mattered."

Yet the memorabilia market we see today is built on the vision and grit of risk-takers, believers, and storytellers. People who recognized that the true value lies beyond the object itself, in the story it carries. Ken Goldin elevated trading cards from dusty collections to billion-dollar auction spectacles watched worldwide. Gary Vaynerchuk anticipated the rise of emotional commerce, showing us that stories and sentiment often sell better than stats alone. Logan Paul reignited a generation's passion for Pokémon, proving that nostalgia is not just a feeling, but a formidable economic force.

Platforms like Rally, Collectable, and Otis have democratized access by allowing everyday fans to own fractions of cultural icons, from Michael Jordan's game-worn shoes to handwritten Beatles lyrics. Meanwhile, Serena Williams and Naomi Osaka have used NFTs and digital memorabilia to bring new voices and underrepresented stories into the spotlight, showing that who tells the story is just as vital as the story itself. Adding to this wave of innovation, Iconic Collectors is launching a memorabilia investment fund, further solidifying collectibles as a serious asset class and opening new pathways for institutional and individual investors alike.

These pioneers aren't merely collectors, they are curators of culture, shaping how we remember and what we value. They remind us that memorabilia aren't fading - they're evolving and expanding into digital, emotional, experiential, and sustainable realms, mirroring the way we live and connect today.

As long as memories matter, so will memorabilia. As long as we care to remember, this market, this culture, this passion - will never die.

The question is, how will *you* harness it?

Appendices

Appendix 1: Iconic Collectors Memorabilia Investment Fund

We are delighted to announce that Iconic collectors (http://iconiccollectors.com) is setting up a memorabilia investment fund whose details are as follows:

Executive Summary

Fund Name: *Iconic Collectors Fund*

The Iconic Collectors Fund is designed to invest in high-value, culturally significant memorabilia, including:

- Graded trading cards (sports & TCG)
- Certified autographs and signed equipment
- Game-used items from iconic athletes
- Vintage comic books and CGC-graded issues
- Rare, sealed toys and collectible IP

Investment Strategy

Iconic Collectors will acquire blue-chip and high-upside memorabilia assets, professionally vault them for security and preservation, and create value through:

- Fractionalization and digital ownership
- Private lending against collateralized assets
- Curated exits via private sales and marquee auctions

Target Assets Under Management- Initial raise of $10M–$50M, with scalable expansion based on asset class performance and investor demand.

Target Internal Rate of Return - Projected returns in the range of 12%–20%, depending on market timing, asset mix, and macroeconomic conditions.

Despite outperforming equities in key timeframes, the memorabilia market remains under allocated in professional portfolios due to:

- Lack of access to high-grade collectibles
- Authentication and provenance challenges
- Storage, insurance, and liquidity barriers
- Fragmented global markets without institutional infrastructure

Iconic collectors will be solving these problems with modern tools, strategic acquisitions, and smart capital deployment to play its role in transforming a passion-led space into a structured investment class.

The conditions have never been more ideal:

- Cultural investing is exploding, especially among Millennials and Gen Z
- Fractionalization, tokenization, and digital vaulting now allow secure, borderless ownership
- Platforms like eBay Vault, Courtyard.io, Goldin Vault, and PWCC have established critical infrastructure
- Investors are actively seeking non-correlated, inflation-hedging alternatives to equities and fixed income

Clearly, the collectible space is entering its institutional era and Iconic Collectors is built to lead it.

The global collectibles market is currently valued at $500B+, encompassing fine art, trading cards, comics, sports memorabilia, toys, and pop culture artifacts. Within that universe:

- The trading card market alone is estimated at $20B+, with strong year-over-year growth

- Digital transformation (e.g., tokenization, marketplaces, AI pricing) is accelerating the liquidity and accessibility of traditionally illiquid assets

- Significant global opportunity in emerging and underpenetrated markets, particularly:

  - Asia (TCG, anime, K-pop, sports)

  - MENA (luxury collectibles, football memorabilia)

  - Latin America (soccer legends, vintage toys, local IP)

This expanding market creates a compelling opportunity for early institutional entry - especially through a professionally managed vehicle like Iconic Collectors Fund.

Target Asset Classes

- Graded sports & non-sports trading cards (PSA/BGS 9.5–10), including GOAT rookies, global legends, and limited-run inserts

- Certified autographed memorabilia, with athlete, entertainer, and IP relevance

- Game-worn and event-used gear, tied to championships, debuts, and iconic moments

- Vintage comics and collectibles, especially CGC-graded blue-chip issues and sealed product

Iconic Collectors will acquire undervalued assets through auctions, private sales, estate buys, and platform partnerships, and leverage elite vaulting partners (e.g., PWCC, Goldin, eBay Vault) for insured, climate-controlled storage. It will offer fractional shares or blockchain-based tokens, enabling global access and liquidity. There will also be a private debt model, issuing collateralized loans against appreciating assets in the vault. As a beneficiary of the fund, you will also get strategic exits through premium resale, direct-to-investor fractional markets, or token liquidity events. This approach of capital appreciation + yield unlocks multiple paths to return.

Competitive Advantage

Iconic Collectors Fund is differentiated by its multi-layer strategy and elite ecosystem access:

- Dual strategy – Equity style returns from asset appreciation plus yield generation via private lending
- Direct access to the world's top grading, storage, and auction platforms (PSA, CGC, Goldin, PWCC, etc.)
- Global sourcing network spanning the U.S., Europe, Asia, MENA, and Latin America
- Tech-first approach - Blockchain integration, digital vaulting, fractionalization, and AI-driven pricing models ensure scalability and modern asset management

Few players in this space can operate across acquisition, finance, and digital distribution the way Iconic Collectors can.

Fund Structure

The fund will be structured as either a traditional LP/ GP model or a tokenized fund offering fractional digital ownership through secure smart contracts. These will be the fees and incentives:

- 5% upfront (used for initial asset acquisition and underwriting)
- 2% annual management fee

- 20% performance fee above a preferred return (hurdle rate)
- Exclusive investor perks - Access to direct purchases, limited-edition merch, and curated celebrity experiences

We are targeting a five to seven-year period. Annual liquidity events will be through resale, secondary markets, or tokenized exits. There will be a 10% targeted dividend (yield-driven via lending & fractional resale) as well as special dividends tied to milestone exits or high-value sales.

Risk Management

The Iconic Collectors Fund is built to mitigate risk at every level through professional-grade tools and controls:

- Third-party authentication via industry-leading grading and verification firms: PSA, BGS, CGC, JSA
- Insured vaulting with providers like Chubb, AXA XL, and Lloyd's of London
- Diversified asset allocation across categories (cards, comics, memorabilia), geographies (U.S., Europe, Asia), and valuation tiers
- Real-time market analytics powered by platforms like CardLadder, Alt, Market Movers, and internal AI-driven models
- Professional custodianship of physical and digital assets to ensure secure handling, reporting, and auditability

The goal is to preserve capital, enhance transparency, and align with the risk expectations of institutional investors.

Exit Strategy

The Iconic Collectors Fund is built for flexible, strategic exits that can adapt to market conditions. We've designed multiple on-ramps and off-ramps to ensure capital doesn't get locked and returns can be realized over time. They include:

Public resale via leading marketplaces

- Goldin Auctions – Premium live and digital auctions
- eBay – Global reach with massive buyer liquidity
- Heritage Auctions – High-end comic and pop culture sales

Fractional exit options

- Offer shares of assets via regulated fractional marketplaces or tokenized platforms
- Enable early-stage liquidity for retail or secondary investors

Debt exit strategy

- Refinance loans with external lenders or institutions
- Sell debt positions or collateralized assets to unlock liquidity

Token exit (optional)

- Leverage NFT-backed platforms for digital sales, international investor reach, and 24/7 liquidity windows

Team & Advisors

The Iconic Collectors Fund brings together a powerhouse team with cross-disciplinary expertise:

- Collectibles experts with decades of experience in trading cards, memorabilia, comics, and authentication
- Financial engineers from private equity, alternative assets, and venture capital

- Legal and compliance advisors with specialization in SEC, FCA, and cross-border fund regulations
- Cultural advisors from the worlds of sports, entertainment, digital media, and influencer marketing - ensuring brand alignment with the next generation of collectors and investors

This blend of expertise ensures cultural relevance and financial rigor.

Financial Projections

Sample Base Case (Five-year Horizon)

- Target IRR: 17%
- Gross Return Multiple: 2.1x
- Annual Cash Yield (from private debt): 8–10%
- Dividend Distribution Target: 10% annually (blend of lending yield + asset resale income)

Returns are modeled conservatively, with upside potential from strategic exits, token liquidity events, and global market expansion.

The cultural asset class is here. If you're ready to lead it - we invite you to join us.

We are currently accepting anchor LPs and strategic partners for the Iconic Collectors Fund.

- Minimum Commitment - $100,000+
- Tiered access is available for early partners, including co-investment rights and exclusive event invitations.

To express interest in the fund or receive the full investor deck, please contact Bobby Rakhit at bobby@rakhitcapital.com.

Appendix 2: Memorabilia Market Data

1. Global memorabilia market by region (Estimates)

REGION	% SHARE	DOLLAR VALUE
United States	40%	$20.4 billion
Europe	25%	$12.75 billion
Asia	20%	$10.2 billion
Latin America	5%	$2.55 billion
Rest of World	10%	$5.1 billion
Global Total	100%	$51.0 billion

2. Approximate average annual returns by asset class

YEAR	SPORTS MEMO-RABILIA	LUXURY WATCHES	S&P 500 (STOCKS)	REAL ESTATE (REITS)	US TREASURY BONDS
2015	12.1%	10.0%	1.4%	2.8%	1.6%
2016	13.3%	8.5%	11.9%	8.6%	1.5%
2017	15.0%	12.3%	21.8%	9.3%	2.3%
2018	9.5%	6.2%	-4.4%	-5.8%	0.9%
2019	16.2%	13.4%	31.5%	28.1%	2.2%
2020	17.5%	14.7%	18.4%	-5.1%	7.7%
2021	18.8%	16.5%	26.9%	40.5%	-2.3%
2022	13.1%	11.1%	-18.1%	-25.1%	-12.0%
2023	15.7%	13.7%	24.2%	11.4%	4.0%
2024	13.9% (est.)	12.0% (est.)	12.6% (est.)	8.1% (est.)	3.5% (est.)

3. Sports memorabilia vs. S&P 500 (2000-2024)

YEAR	SPORTS MEMORABILIA (%)	S&P 500 (%)
2000	5.5%	-10.1%
2001	6%	-13%
2002	7.2%	-23.4%
2003	8%	26.4%
2004	6.8%	9%
2005	7.5%	3%
2006	9%	13.6%
2007	8.5%	3.5%
2008	7.8%	-38.5%
2009	10%	23.5%
2010	8%	12. %8
2011	9.5%	0%
2012	11%	13.4%
2013	12.2%	29.6%
2014	12.1%	11.4%
2015	13.3%	1.4%
2016	15%	11.9%
2017	9.5%	21.8%
2018	16.2%	-4.4%
2019	17.5%	31.5%
2020	18.8%	18.4%
2021	13.1%	26.9%
2022	15.7%	-18.1%
2023	13.9%	24.2%
2024	14.5%	12.6%

Appendix 3: Where to Buy Memorabilia

1. Top Auctions in the world

AUCTION HOUSE	LOCATION	SPECIALTIES	OFFICIAL WEBSITE
Goldin Auctions	Runnemede, New Jersey, USA	Sports memorabilia, trading cards, pop culture collectibles	https://www.goldin.co
Heritage Auctions	Dallas, Texas, USA	Sports collectibles, comics, coins, fine art, historical memorabilia	https://www.ha.com
Sotheby's	New York, London, Hong Kong	Fine art, luxury goods, rare collectibles (incl. sports and pop culture items)	https://www.sothebys.com
Christie's	New York, London, Hong Kong	Fine art, watches, rare memorabilia, historical items	https://www.christies.com
Lelands	Long Island, New York, USA	Sports memorabilia, vintage cards, game-used gear	https://www.lelands.com

Robert Edward Auctions (REA)	Chester, New Jersey, USA	Baseball memorabilia, vintage cards, historical sports artifacts	https://www. robertedwardauctions. com
PWCC Marketplace	Portland, Oregon, USA	Digital and physical trading cards, sports card investment lots	https://www. pwccmarketplace.com
Bonhams	London, Los Angeles, Hong Kong	High-end art, cars, historical collectibles, books, some sports memorabilia	https://www.bonhams. com
RR Auction	Boston, Massachusetts, USA	Autographs, space memorabilia, pop culture, presidential and sports signatures	https://www.rrauction. com
Classic Auctions	Quebec, Canada	Ice hockey memorabilia, vintage cards, jerseys, Canadian sports collectibles	https://www. classicauctions.net

2. Top Dealers in the World

DEALER NAME	LOCATION	SPECIALTY	WEBSITE
Exclusive Memorabilia	UK (Devon)	Signed sports memorabilia	https://www.exclusivememorabilia.com
Steiner Sports	USA (New York)	Authenticated sports memorabilia	https://www.sportsmemorabilia.com
Goldin	USA (New Jersey)	Premium trading cards and signed items	https://www.goldin.co
Upper Deck Authenticated	USA (California)	Autographed collectibles	https://www.upperdeckstore.com
Icons.com	UK	FIFA-licensed signed football items	https://www.icons.com
The Bootroom Collection	UAE (Dubai)	Signed football memorabilia	https://www.bootroomcollection.com
Signed Memorabilia 4U	UK	Entertainment & music memorabilia	https://www.signedmemorabilia4u.com
Fanatics Authentic	USA	Licensed NFL, MLB, and NBA items	https://www.fanaticsauthentic.com
Camel Comics	UAE (online)	Comics and pop culture collectibles	https://www.camelcomics.com

3. Online Auctions and Marketplaces

AUCTION PLATFORM	WEBSITE	SPECIALTIES	NOTABLE FEATURES
PWCC Marketplace	https://www.pwccmarketplace.com	Trading cards, investment-grade collectibles	Vault storage, private sales, and weekly/monthly auctions
SCP Auctions	https://www.scpauctions.com	Historic sports memorabilia, game-worn gear	Exclusive athlete and estate collections; premium client base
Lelands	https://www.lelands.com	Vintage cards, sports gear, historical memorabilia	The original sports memorabilia auction house; seasonal events
eBay	https://www.ebay.com	All memorabilia types (cards, autographs, jerseys, etc.)	Global reach, seller flexibility, but requires authentication diligence
MySlabs	https://www.myslabs.com	Slabbed cards, comics, sealed wax boxes	Peer-to-peer marketplace with low seller fees; niche but growing
CertifiedLink	https://www.certifiedlink.com	Comic books, cards, vintage collectibles	Certified-only items; curated listings

Classic Auctions	https://www.classicauctions.net	Ice hockey memorabilia, Canadian sports gear	Strong hockey focus; bilingual (English/French) platform
Pristine Auction	https://www.pristineauction.com	Daily auctions for autographs, jerseys, collectibles	Easy-to-use interface; daily sales; affordable entry points
Iconic Auctions	https://www.iconicauctions.com	Signed memorabilia, autographs, entertainment items	Frequent themed auctions; autograph authentication partnerships

Appendix 4: List of Conventions, Conferences and Trade Shows

CONVENTION NAME	LOCATION (S)	DATES (2025)	FOCUS AREA	KEY HIGHLIGHTS	WEBSITE
National Sports Collectors Convention (NSCC)	Rotating U.S. cities (e.g., Chicago)	July 30 – August 3	Sports Collectibles	Premier event for dealers, athletes, private trades, live deals	https://www.nsccshow.com
Fanatics Fest	New York City (Javits Center)	June 20–22	Sports, Pop Culture, Cards	Blends pop culture, athletes, card breaks; dubbed "Coachella for Collectibles"	https://www.fanaticsfest.com
Collect-A-Con (Touring)	Houston, Orlando, Chicago, Denver, Miami	April–November	Cards, Comics, Vintage Toys	500+ dealers, live music, celebrity guests	https://www.collectacon.com

WonderCon	Anaheim, CA	March 28–30	Comics, Pop Culture	Creator meet-and-greets, exclusive merchandise	https://www.comic-con.org/wca
CT HorrorFest	Stamford & Hartford, CT	May 3–4, Sept 20–21	Horror Memorabilia	Horror icons, niche memorabilia, collectors of horror-themed media	https://www.cthorrorfest.com
San Diego Comic-Con (SDCC)	San Diego, CA	July 24–27	Comics, Pop Culture, Limited Editions	World's largest pop culture convention, exclusive releases, major franchise events	https://www.comic-con.org
New York Comic Con (NYCC)	New York City, NY	October 9–12	Comics, Toys, Pop Culture	Major industry presence, exclusives, celebrity signings	https://www.newyorkcomiccon.com

Toy Fair New York	New York City, NY	February 14–17	Toys & Memorabilia (Industry Focus)	Annual showcase of the latest trends and collectibles	https://www.toyfairny.com
Power-Con	Columbus, OH	August (TBD)	Vintage Toys (He-Man, Transformers)	Specialized in 80s/90s toy collectibles and auctions	https://www.thepower-con.com
RetroGameCon / Classic Gaming Expo	Syracuse, Portland, Las Vegas (varies)	Varies by year	Retro Video Games	Rare gaming memorabilia, arcade, graded games	https://www.retrogamecon.com

This table captures the most influential conventions and expos in 2025 that are shaping the growth of the global collectibles market. These events not only serve as marketplaces but also as cultural epicenters.

Appendix 5: Grading and Certification Information

This table compares leading trading card grading companies by resale value, processing speed, subgrade availability, and best use cases. Star ratings reflect general market perception of resale value, not the quality of service.

GRADER	RESALE VALUE	PROCESSING SPEED	SUB-GRADE AVAILABILITY	BEST FOR
PSA	Highest	Moderate	No	Sports cards, Trading Card Games (TCG), Vintage cards
BGS (Beckett Grading Services)	High	Slow	Yes	High-end sports cards
SGC	Moderate	Fast	No	Vintage cards
CGC	Moderate	Fast	Yes	Trading Card Games (Pokémon, Magic: The Gathering)
HGA	Lower	Moderate	Yes	Display quality, modern cards
Others (ACE, GMA, etc.)	Entry-level	Varies	Varies	Budget-friendly grading or personal collections

Appendix 6: Budgeting Tools

Editable worksheet for budgeting - Memorabilia Budgeting Tools

Appendix 7: Most Expensive Memorabilia of All Time

1. The most expensive sports memorabilia items of all time

ITEM	SPORT	PRICE (USD)	SALE YEAR	ADDITIONAL INFORMATION
Babe Ruth's 1932 "Called Shot" Jersey	Baseball	$24.12M	2024	Worn during Ruth's legendary "called shot" home run in the 1932 World Series. Sold at Heritage Auctions.
1952 Topps Mickey Mantle Baseball Card	Baseball	$12.6M	2022	Mint+ 9.5 graded card. One of the rarest and most iconic cards in sports history.
Michael Jordan's 1998 NBA Finals Game 1 Jersey	Basketball (NBA)	$10.1M	2022	Worn in Game 1 of his last Finals with the Bulls. Sold at Sotheby's.
Diego Maradona's 1986 "Hand of God" Shirt	Soccer (Football)	$9.28M	2022	Worn during the infamous quarterfinal match vs. England. Auctioned by Steve Hodge.
1892 Olympic Games Manifesto	Historical Document	$8.8M	2019	Pierre de Coubertin's original document founding the modern Olympic Games.

Lionel Messi's 2022 World Cup Match-Worn Shirt Set (6 shirts)	Soccer (Football)	$7.8M	2023	Worn by Messi in various 2022 World Cup matches. Sold via Sotheby's.
Muhammad Ali's 1974 "Rumble in the Jungle" Gloves	Boxing	$6.8M	2022	Worn in Ali's iconic victory over George Foreman in Zaire. Purchased by Jim Irsay.
Babe Ruth's 1920 Yankees Jersey	Baseball	$5.6M	2019	One of the earliest surviving Ruth jerseys, worn with the Yankees.
Muhammad Ali's 1975 "Thriller in Manila" Fight Shorts	Boxing	$4–6M (est.)	2023	Worn in the legendary bout against Joe Frazier in Manila. Auction estimate from Time.com.
Kobe Bryant's 1996–97 Rookie Season Jersey	Basketball (NBA)	$3.7M	2021	Signed and game-worn rookie jersey, sold in early 2021.

2. The most expensive entertainment memorabilia of all time

ITEM	CATEGORY	PRICE	YEAR OF SALE	ADDITIONAL INFORMATION
Dorothy's Ruby Slippers	Movie Props (The Wizard of Oz)	$32 Million	2015	Worn by Judy Garland in *The Wizard of Oz*. Sold at Heritage Auctions.

Marilyn Monroe's "Happy Birthday" Dress	Movie Costume (Hollywood)	$4.8 Million	2016	Worn by Monroe during her famous 1962 performance for President John F. Kennedy's birthday celebration. Sold at Julien's Auctions.
The Batmobile (1966)	Movie Prop (Batman)	$4.2 Million	2013	The original Batmobile used in the 1966 *Batman* TV series sold at Barrett-Jackson.
The DeLorean from *Back to the Future*	Movie Prop (Back to the Future)	$4.1 Million	2022	Auctioned by Barrett-Jackson.
Michael Jackson's "Bad" Tour Jacket	Music Memorabilia	$2.2 Million	2019	Worn by Michael Jackson during his 1988 "Bad" tour. Sold at Julien's Auctions. (The sale was part of Jackson's personal memorabilia collection.)
Jimi Hendrix's Woodstock Guitar	Music Memorabilia	$2 Million	2020	The guitar Jimi Hendrix played during his legendary 1969 Woodstock performance. It was sold by Sotheby's.

The Original Star Wars Boba Fett Helmet	Movie Prop (Star Wars)	$1.5 Million	2022	One of the original helmets worn by Boba Fett in *Star Wars: The Empire Strikes Back*. This helmet was sold at Bonhams.
Elvis Presley's 1976 Stutz Blackhawk Car	Music Memorabilia	$1.4 Million	2022	Elvis Presley's personal 1976 Stutz Blackhawk car, which he owned for several years, was sold at an auction by RM Sotheby's.
Marlon Brando's Godfather Jacket	Movie Costume (The Godfather)	$1.02 Million	2016	The famous jacket worn by Brando as Vito Corleone in *The Godfather* was sold at a Sotheby's auction.
Audrey Hepburn's "Breakfast at Tiffany's" Dress	Movie Costume (Breakfast at Tiffany's)	$1.0 Million	2006	The iconic dress worn by Audrey Hepburn in *Breakfast at Tiffany's* was sold at a Christie's auction. The dress has since become a symbol of the classic film's glamour.

3. Most expensive historical & political memorabilia of all time

ITEM	TYPE	PRICE	YEAR OF SALE	ADDITIONAL INFO
U.S. Constitution (First Edition)	Document	$43.2 million	2021	One of only 13 surviving original copies of the U.S. Constitution. Sold at Sotheby's to cryptocurrency entrepreneur Kurt D. Peterson.
Abraham Lincoln's Signed 1863 Emancipation Proclamation	Document	$3.7 million	2012	An 1863 Emancipation Proclamation signed by Abraham Lincoln. Sold at Sotheby's.
George Washington's Signed Letter	Document	$3.4 million	2018	A letter signed by George Washington, the first president of the United States. Sold at Sotheby's.
Berlin Wall Fragments	Artifact	$1.5 million	2015	Pieces of the Berlin Wall, symbolizing the fall of the wall in 1989. Sold at Bonhams.
Winston Churchill Signed Photograph	Photograph	$400,000	2017	A signed photograph of Winston Churchill, famous for his leadership during WWII. Sold at Bonhams.

Franklin D. Roosevelt's Signed WWII Speech	Document	$276,000	2019	A signed manuscript of Roosevelt's "Day of Infamy" speech after Pearl Harbor. Sold at Sotheby's.
John F. Kennedy's Inaugural Ball Tickets	Campaign Memorabilia	$75,000	2017	Original tickets to John F. Kennedy's 1961 Inaugural Ball. Sold at RR Auction.
Abraham Lincoln's Blood-Stained Gloves	Artifact (Personal)	$68,000	2007	A pair of gloves worn by Abraham Lincoln on the night of his assassination. Sold at Heritage Auctions.
Abraham Lincoln's 1860 Campaign Ribbon	Campaign Memorabilia	$40,000	2018	A rare 1860 campaign ribbon from Lincoln's first presidential run. Sold at Heritage Auctions.
John F. Kennedy's Presidential Inauguration Invitation	Campaign Memorabilia	$16,000	2017	The original invitation to JFK's 1961 Presidential Inauguration. Sold at RR Auction.

4. Most expensive pop-culture memorabilia of all time

ITEM	TYPE	PRICE	YEAR OF SALE	ADDITIONAL INFO
Action Comics #1 (Superman's First Appearance)	Comic Book	$3.2 million	2014	Considered one of the most valuable comics in the world.
Super Mario Bros. NES Sealed Copy	Video Game	$2 million	2021	A sealed copy of the classic game, graded 9.8 A+ by Wata Games.
The Amazing Spider-Man #1 (First Appearance)	Comic Book	$1.1 million	2011	The debut comic of Spider-Man, one of the most beloved characters in comic book history.
Star Wars Stormtrooper Helmet (Limited Edition)	Merchandise	$500,000	2017	A limited-edition replica of the iconic Stormtrooper helmet from Star Wars.
First Edition Charizard Pokémon Card	Trading Cards (Pokémon)	$420,000	2021	A rare First Edition holographic Charizard card, one of the most iconic and valuable Pokémon cards in existence.
1959 Barbie Doll (Vintage)	Toys/Dolls	$300,000	2018	The rarest and most valuable version of the first-ever Barbie doll.

First Edition GI Joe Action Figure (1964)	Toys/Action Figures	$200,000	2021	A rare first-edition GI Joe action figure, one of the first action figures ever made.
Limited Edition Harry Potter Wand	Merchandise	$150,000	2020	A limited-edition wand from the Harry Potter franchise.
Boba Fett Action Figure (1978)	Toys/Action Figures	$110,000	2015	A rare 1978 Star Wars Boba Fett action figure in its original packaging.
The 1977 Star Wars Action Figures Set (12)	Toys/Action Figures	$27,000	2017	A collection of 12 original Star Wars action figures still in near-mint condition, sealed in their original packaging.

Appendix 8: Other Important Information

1. Memorabilia books

Collecting Baseball Memorabilia by Dan Zachofsky - A practical guide for collectors of autographed baseball items, offering advice on obtaining autographs, designing memorabilia displays, and navigating online auctions.

The Great American Baseball Card Flipping, Trading and Bubble Gum Book by Brendan C. Boyd & Fred C. Harris - A nostalgic look at baseball cards from the 1950s, featuring humorous profiles of players and insights into the culture of card collecting during that era.

Do Not Sell at Any Price: The Wild, Obsessive Hunt for the World's Rarest 78rpm Records by Amanda Petrusich - An exploration into the world of rare 78rpm vinyl records, delving into the passion and obsession of collectors seeking these elusive items.

The Coin Collector's Survival Manual by Scott A. Travers - A comprehensive guide for coin collectors, covering topics from grading and authentication to investment strategies and market trends.

Miller's Antiques Encyclopedia by Judith Miller - Often referred to as the "bible" of antiques, this encyclopedia provides detailed information on a wide range of antiques and collectibles, including identification, dating, and valuation.

The Business of Antiques: How to Succeed in the Antiques World by Wayne Jordan - A practical guide for those interested in the business side of antiques, offering insights into trading, valuation, and building a successful antiques business.

Star Wars: The Ultimate Action Figure Collection by Steve Sansweet - A comprehensive guide to nearly 2,500 Star Wars action figures released between 1978 and 2012, detailing their history and significance in the collectible market.

Boy Scouts of America Scout Stuff: A Centennial History of Scouting Memorabilia by DK Publishing - A richly illustrated book celebrating over 100 years of Boy Scouts memorabilia, including patches, uniforms, and camping gear, highlighting the evolution of scouting collectibles.

2. Useful websites Institute for Accreditation for investment professionals - https://www.cfainstitute.org/

Appendix 9: Key Jargon and Buzzwords

Appraisal - A professional assessment of an item's market value, usually for insurance, sale, or investment purposes.

Authentication - The process of verifying an item's legitimacy, often performed by third-party experts or companies.

Autograph Letter Signed (ALS) - A letter written and signed by a notable figure (fully handwritten).

Blockchain provenance - Using blockchain technology to verify the ownership and history of a collectible- tamper-proof.

Blue chip collectible - A stable, historically valuable item considered a safe long-term investment (e.g., Babe Ruth-signed ball).

Broadside - A one-sided historical poster or public notice-often political or event-related.

Buyer's Premium - An extra percentage added to the hammer price, paid by the buyer to the auction house. It typically ranges from 10% to 25%, depending on the platform or item.

COA (Certificate of Authenticity) - A document verifying that an item is genuine, typically issued by a reputable dealer or studio.

Collectible - Any item people collect for its rarity or appeal (broader than memorabilia- includes stamps, coins, cards, etc.).

Custodied asset - An item stored and managed by a third party on behalf of fractional owners.

Digital twin - A virtual representation of a physical collectible, often tied to an NFT.

Document Signed (DS) - A printed or typed document signed by a notable figure.

Ephemeral - Paper-based historical memorabilia such as tickets, posters, or pamphlets.

Event-worn - Worn during a public appearance or pre-game, but not during actual play.

Fractional ownership - A model where multiple investors share ownership of a single high-value collectible. It allows people to invest in rare items without purchasing the whole asset.

Game-used - Items used by an athlete in play but not necessarily worn (e.g., balls, bats).

Game-worn - Apparel or gear worn by an athlete during a game (most valuable type).

Grade - A score (usually 1–10 or 1–100) that evaluates the condition of a collectible, often given by PSA, Beckett, CGC, etc.

Hall of Fame (HOF) - Additional hand-written notes on signed memorabilia noting Hall of Fame induction or achievements.

Hammer Price - The final bid price of an item at auction before additional fees (such as the buyer's premium) are applied.

Hero prop - A main, high-detail prop handled by actors on-screen- more valuable than background pieces.

Holy Grail - A term used by collectors to describe the most coveted, iconic, and rare item in a particular category. It's the dream acquisition for serious collectors.

Jersey tagging - Labels inside sports jerseys that verify origin and use (e.g., season, game date).

Limited Edition (LE) - An item that is produced in restricted quantities. Limited editions are often individually numbered (e.g., 24/100), making them more collectible due to their scarcity.

Liquidity - The ease of buying/selling an asset. Many collectibles are considered illiquid.

Manuscript - A handwritten document- often literary, political, or scientific in nature.

Memorabilia - Physical objects connected to famous people, events, or moments- collected for sentimental, historical, or monetary value.

Mint Condition - Describes an item that is in flawless, original condition. It shows no signs of wear, damage, or deterioration, as if it just came from the factory.

Near Mint (NM) - Indicates an item that is almost perfect but may have minor flaws such as slight wear or faint marks. It is still considered highly collectible.

NFT (non-fungible token) - A unique digital asset representing ownership of an item or moment, sometimes linked to physical memorabilia.

Player-issued - Equipment given to a player but never used in a game- less valuable than game-used.

Premium Item - A top-tier collectible with strong demand and exceptional provenance.

Provenance - The documented history of an item's ownership, used to establish authenticity and value.

Repro (Reproduction) - A replica, often made for fans or secondary use- not original.

Reserve Price - The minimum price a seller is willing to accept for an item in auction. If bidding does not reach the reserve, the item is not sold.

Rookie-card - A player's first-ever trading card- usually the most valuable in the long term.

Screen-worn - Costumes or props used in film or television production.

Secondary market - Where collectors resell items- auctions, online platforms, or private deals.

Set-used - Items used during filming, even if not visible on screen.

Slabbing - Sealing collectibles (like trading cards) in protective cases with grading labels.

Tokenization - Converting physical memorabilia into tradable digital tokens (fractional or full).

Virtual Vault - A digital viewing/storage experience for physical items kept off-site, often used in fractional platforms.

References

Admin. (2024, July 30). *The world's most watched sports - sport for business*. Sport for

Business. https://sportforbusiness.com/the-worlds-most-watched-sports/

ancient relics for sale - Search Videos. (n.d.). https://www.bing.com/videos/riverview/relatedvideo?q=anient+reics forsale&mid=8D241A5985EA4FEE57FD241A5985EA4 EE57FF&mcid=447DA9C84B144FDF9437C4FC3FF2 2CF&FORM=VIRE

Cole, J. (2024, June 5). Market Trends: The impact of player popularity - BlockApps Inc. *BlockApps Inc*. https://blockapps.net/blog/market-trends-the-impact-of-player-popularity/

Collectibles Market Size, Share and Trends Report, 2030. (n.d.). https://www.grandviewresearch.com/industry-analysis/collectibles-market-report

Dodgson, C. (2024, May 16). *How & Where to Sell My Sports Memorabilia; Why is it Important? - The Pristine Auction Blog*. The Pristine Auction Blog. https://blog.pristineauction.com/blog/where-how-to-sell-sports-memorabilia

Dorothy's Ruby Slippers From 'The Wizard of Oz' Sell for $32.5 Million at Heritage Auctions to. . . (n.d.). https://entertainment.ha.com/heritage-auctions-press-releases-and-news/dorothy-s-ruby-slippers-from-the-wizard-of-oz-sell-for-32.5-million-at-heritage-auctions-to-become-world-s-most-valuable-movie-memorabilia.s?releaseId=5122

Gherghelas, S. (2024). *DAPP Industry Report 2023*. DappRadar. https://dappradar.com/blog/dapp-industry-report-2023-defi-nft-web3-games

Howcroft, E. (2022). *NFT sales hit $25 billion in 2021, but growth shows signs of slowing*. Reuters. https://www.reuters.com/markets/europe/nft-sales-hit-25-billion-2021-growth-shows-signs-slowing-2022-01-10/

Jacobo, J. (2018, May 14). *Lincoln's hat, bloody gloves among items potentially at risk for auction to pay debt.* ABC News. https://abcnews.go.com/US/lincolns-hat-bloody-gloves-items-potentially-risk-auction/story?id=55106203

McClintock, P. (2024, January 4). 2023 Box Office: Global revenue clears estimated $33.9B in 31 percent gain over prior year. *The Hollywood Reporter.* https://www.hollywoodreporter.com/movies/movie-news/2023-global-revenue-box-office-1235779026/

NAICS OD5071. (2024). *Online Antiques & Collectibles sales in the US - Market size (2005–2030).* IbisWorld. https://www.ibisworld.com/united-states/market-size/online-antiques-collectibles-sales/5071/

North America Sports Collectibles and Memorabilia Market. (n.d.). https://www.marketdecipher.com/report/north-america-sports-memorabilia-market

Reports, V. M. (2025). Future of Sports Memorabilia Collectibles Market in the United States | Market Trends & 2025 Forecast. In *Verified Market Reports.* https://www.verifiedmarketreports.com/product/sports-memorabilia-collectibles-market/

Sedacca, M. (2022, August 28). Mickey Mantle baseball card sells for record-smashing $12.6M. *New York Post.* https://nypost.com/2022/08/28/mickey-mantle-sold-for-record-12-6-million/

Seideman, D. (2018a, September 19). *Tech entrepreneur determines first estimate of U.S. sports memorabilia market: $5.4 billion.* Forbes. https://www.forbes.com/sites/davidseideman/2018/09/19/tech-entrepreneur-determines-first-true-estimate-of-sports-memorabilia-market-5-4-billion/

Seideman, D. (2018b, December 18). *A beginner's guide to selling your collectibles in auctions.* Forbes. https://www.forbes.com/sites/davidseideman/2018/12/18/my-tried-and-true-secrets-to-selling-your-collectibles-in-auctions/

Shields, A. (2021). *The world's most expensive pieces of sporting memorabilia.* Casino.org. https://www.casino.org/blog/most-expensive-sporting-memorabilia/

Sports Memorabilia Collectibles Market Size, Share, Trends. (2024a, October 9). Verified Market Research. https://www.verifiedmarketresearch.com/product/sports-memorabilia-collectibles-market/

Sports Memorabilia Collectibles Market Size, Share, Trends. (2024b, October 9). Verified Market Research. https://www.verifiedmarketresearch.com/product/sports-memorabilia-collectibles-market/

Statista. (2025, March 3). *Quarterly Netflix subscribers count worldwide 2013-2024.* https://www.statista.com/statistics/250934/quarterly-number-of-netflix-streaming-subscribers-worldwide/

Total Prestige Magazine. (2020, July 10). *Most expensive memorabilia ever sold.* https://www.totalprestigemagazine.com/most-expensive-memorabilia-ever-sold/

Vigderman, A. (2024, November 20). *NFT Awareness and Adoption Report.* Security.org. https://www.security.org/digital-security/nft-market-analysis/

Zdanowicz, C. (2020). *Abraham Lincoln's Lock of Hair sells for more than $81,000 at auction.* CNN. https://edition.cnn.com/2020/09/14/us/abraham-lincoln-hair-auction-trnd/index.html

Zoting, S. (2025, January 31). *Video games market size to hit USD 721.77 billion by 2034.* https://www.precedenceresearch.com/video-game-market

Note- The source of all images is cited, where known, and most images are publicly available.